A GARDEN SUPPER TONIGHT

Barbara Swell

ISBN 9781883206598   Order No. NGB-836
Library of Congress Control Number: 2009926759
©2009 by Native Ground Books & Music, Inc. Asheville, North Carolina
International Copyright Secured. All Rights Reserved.

WELCOME TO MY GARDEN

How did Americans get to the place where we require a book to teach us how to eat with the seasons? So pondered my gardening friend, Betty, when I told her about this seasonal cookbook in the works. Good question, Betty. In our grandmother's day, everyone with any yard at all, had a garden and grew at least some of their family's food. What you didn't grow, you bought from the local store that carried eggs, milk, produce and meat from nearby farms. It wasn't until after WWII that we depended on refrigerated shipping, and even then, the expensive produce from distant climates neither looked nor tasted good. As my grandmother always said, "If you want to be a good cook, you have to know what good food looks and tastes like." Of course she and my grandfather grew a gorgeous garden and owned the grocery store in Salem, West Virginia. She knew what good food tasted like 'cause that's all they carried. Asparagus in April, cucumbers in July, corn in August. You could get a lamb shank for your Easter dinner as soon as Grandfather butchered the lamb out back of the store.

Somehow, in the decades following the war, we lost our collective grip on what good food is supposed to taste like and we sacrificed flavor for convenience. Unless you grow tomatoes yourself, you don't know that the only tomato worth eating is one whose seeds have been passed from hand to hand and has so much flavor and color you could cry. Don't get me started on corn. OK, just this one little thing. Nowadays, you can get corn any time of year and it's actually sweet. The sort of sweet that comes in a little blue packet of sweetener and is crunchier than a fresh-plucked Winesap apple. Not corn, really. Corn is supposed to be tender and sweet the day you pick it like, say, that nectar you pull from the guts of a honeysuckle flower.

Not only did we give up on the taste of our food beginning some fifty years ago, we all but lost our regional varieties of produce and animal breeds there for a while. Maybe you know someone like my friend, Alma. She's long since passed, but folks still talk longingly about her pickled potato patch beans whose seeds had been in her family for generations. Alma wouldn't settle for less than the best bean adapted to the North Carolina mountains where she lived, and

WELCOME TO MY GARDEN

fortunately for us, her family and friends continue to grow them. Now you can find potato patch beans like Alma's through seed saving organizations along with many other similarly treasured varieties of vegetables and fruits adapted to your own locale.

There's much ado these days about eating local, sustainably produced meats, vegetables and grains. We want our farmers to earn a living wage and our food to be grown without bringing harm to workers, the environment and us in the process. I won't reinvent that wheel, but it does make sense to eat food whose story we know. Shouldn't we be paying just as much attention to the food we serve our families as we do to the boys who want to court our teenage daughters?

It's easy to know the story of your food if you grow and preserve your own, or if you buy from your local farmers, or from groceries that let you know where their produce originates. What's not as easy is making the choice of where to spend your food dollars because good food costs more. It always has.

I had so much fun writing this book. The vintage recipes were tested with produce I grew, pilfered, plucked, gathered, caught or bought from our local Asheville, North Carolina farmers. The flours were milled regionally and the grains similar to what would have been available a century ago. I used locally made cheeses as well as raw milk, eggs and meats from my friends' animals. With family and friends, I gathered, on a moment's notice, wild huckleberries from Blue Ridge mountaintops; raspberries, blueberries and strawberries from u-pick farms; pears, cherries and plums from neighborhood trees; blackberries, black raspberries and wineberries from roadside brambles. Antique apples from our historic mountain cabin landed into pies, cider, apple sauce, and the dehydrator. I canned, dried, froze, pickled and jammed all summer and fall to create the winter recipes from the preserved goods.

Some of the recipes herein will work for you and some won't because tastes, measurements, ingredients, cooking equipment and methods have changed over time. But I do hope you'll consider that an asparagus is best eaten in April when it sings a crunchy sweet song that you savor again and again and again ... enough to do you till next April!

How to
Use This Book

learned to cook at the elbows of elder-ladies and I don't measure. The grandmothers, mothers, and aunts of generations past didn't measure either. Unless you call "about two cups of flour from the red patterned teacup with the cracked handle" measuring. Instead, I learned to add enough flour to make a soft dough and then that soft ball of dough got plopped into my floured hands so I could feel it. In this book, you'll find two kinds of recipes from America's past:

1. Those recipes with recognizable measurements from the ever-efficient and often uppity domestic cooking school ladies that somehow found their way into the kitchens of your average everyday housewife via ladies magazines.

2. And then there are the recipes that don't include much in the way of specifics about how to make the recipe, these coming from the women that actually could cook a memorable spread of wholesome tasty food fresh from their garden or their neighbor's farm. These recipes I found in handwritten cooking journals, magazines like *Woman's Farm Journal*, community cookbooks or from yellowed newspaper cooking column clippings between the 1850s and 1930s.

I prefer the recipes from "the ladies who don't measure," and I hope that even if you don't prepare these recipes, you'll enjoy reading them. Just a reminder: **THE INSTRUCTIONS AND MEASURE-MENTS FOR VINTAGE RECIPES IN THIS BOOK ARE NOT PRE-CISE!!!** Well, heck, no recipe in this book has an exacting bone in its body because I don't even have measuring cups, and I often bake in a wood cookstove whose temperature gauge is how long it takes to singe the hairs off my arm. If you need more guidance, consult an instructive cookbook. Better yet, find a good old-fashioned make-do cook with an abundant kitchen garden who can help you with these recipes and maybe she'll share some of her own favorites as well.

> The historic recipes in this book are presented to you as found ... spelling and measuring errors and all. They'll be in shadowed boxes like this one. If I update or change anything, I'll let you know in an author's note. The undated recipes are contemporary.

Alrighty now, go tie on your apron and let's have some fun!

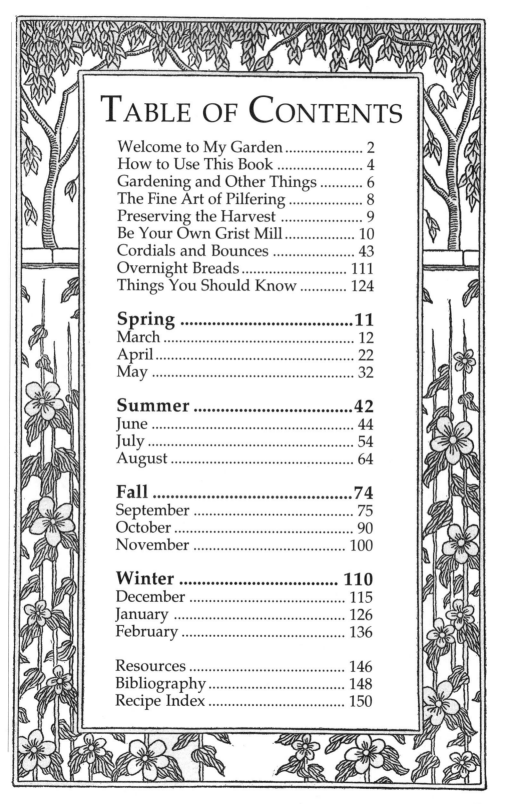

TABLE OF CONTENTS

GARDENING
and Other Things

The first thing to decide about a home garden is that you are going to have one. *~Southern Ruralist* February, 1925

HAVE YOU A GARDEN?

"HAVE you a garden? Just a little homey garden that you plant and tend yourself, and find joy in? Then you are feeling with me the little wakings of interest that come anew with each early springtime when the birds outside your window greet the dawn with such animated chatter, and a soft something in the air sends an electric impulse to your blood, with the realization that the time is come again to garden! Perhaps, like me, you have thought I cannot give the time to it again; but the hint in the sky, the suggestion in the air, the busy beginnings of the birds, my gardening ear is alert, and all suddenly I am full of zest and zeal! Is it so with you?" *~ American Cookery*, May 1919

Yes, have you a little garden! There are record numbers of folks gardening now as grocery prices soar and we care more about the food our family

consumes. If you're new to gardening, there are lots of opportunities to learn the particulars from county extension programs, books, grower's schools, and your friends who grow.

HELPING HOOVER IN OUR U. S. SCHOOL GARDEN

If you don't have a space for a garden, consider participating in or organizing a community garden. (See resources, page 146 for support.) School gardens are growing in numbers, and schools often need community members to mentor, co-garden and harvest the produce when school is out for the summer.

GARDENING
and Other Things

NEW-TURNED SOIL

I like the sight of the springing grasses, the sound of the robins in wayside trees;
I love the feel of each wind that passes, the taste of greens, & such things as these,
I like the thrill of the springtime spirit; the daisied way that my footsteps trod;
But more than these, and the best, or near it, I like the smell of the new turned sod!

I like the sight of a garden, golden, with open tulips and daffodils;
And just behind it a farmhouse olden, set in a girdle of spruce-green hills.
I like the sound of the country's voices, I count but pleasure its sternest toil;
For I am glad and my heart rejoices, in the pungent smell of the new turned soil!

~L.M. Thornton *Farm and Home Magazine* March 15, 1917

Of course, not everyone is able to, nor wants to grow a garden. You can still eat seasonally and support your local farmers either by frequenting roadside farm stands, farmer's tailgate markets, or by purchasing a CSA share. Community Supported Agriculture (CSA) consumers buy produce directly from the farmer in the form of "shares." Each share is a box of vegetables and sometimes other products like honey and jam that is delivered to a convenient pickup place once a week during the growing season. You subscribe in the winter and the farmer uses a portion of the money to prepare for the farming season. Here in Western North Carolina, we have lots of farms that offer CSA's. Shares can sell out early on, so plan ahead. You learn quickly how to feast on great produce when it's plentiful and then you move on to the next in-season gem. If all goes well, you'll eventually decide to only eat tomatoes, corn, cucumbers, etc. when they're in season in your region because the engineered varieties that stand up to shipping just aren't good enough any more.

THE FINE ART OF PILFERING

But the fruit that falls without shaking
Indeed is too mellow for me.
~I Go A-Marketing, 1900

No, I don't mean pilfering as in palming produce at the local farmer's market. I'm talking about taking windfall fruits and the occasional zucchini off the hands of your grateful neighbors with their permission. Still, it's a thrill to get the phone call from your friend who says the plums are ready to be plucked and the tree owner is happy to share. Sadly, there are some who would rather buy cherries from a can than pick and pit from their own trees. Others enjoy the bounty from their trees, but don't have time to preserve the harvest. And then there's me. Always happy to take what you don't want. I'll make your fruit into jam, cordials, wine, pies, cakes, fritters and then give it back to you. There are plenty of "me-s" out there.

Pilfer-queen, Brookes, picks cherries

This season, I planted a pilfering orchard of ten fruit trees alongside my garden that faces the road running through the neighborhood. In about three years, our neighbors can walk by my garden and grab a Green Gage plum, Sheepnose apple or Moonglow pear to munch on as they walk down the street. Just think, if everybody planted a fruit tree or two in their front yard to share with their neighbors, what a feast we'd all have!

Pilfered plums

How about donating your surplus produce to a gleaning organization that serves the hungry in your community? They'll come out and pick what you can't use. (See resources page 146.)

PRESERVING THE HARVEST

This is GOOD storage

Courtesy Library of Congress

You want to feel rich? I'm not talking about Wall Street, I'm talking about a gold mine right in your own home. Your pantry shelves lined with your canned, dried and pickled summer harvest. If you don't grow your own, contact your local farmers to see if they offer discounted prices on bulk quantities of your favorites. Those wild fruits you picked make terrific jams and jellies. Don't forget to ask your neighbors if you can glean the "leavings" of their fruit trees. Most are more than happy to share.

You'll find recipes for dried, fermented, frozen, canned, and jammed foods in these chapters, but when it comes to canning, I'd advise you to take the preserving course from your local county extension office. Improperly canned food can kill you. Some communities have working neighborhood canneries staffed by professionals who can help you.

DON'T

Preserving the harvest is always more fun when you do it with friends, so make a party of it, then celebrate with a good old-fashioned harvest feast.

BE YOUR OWN
GRIST MILL

You can't even compare store-bought grains to those you grind yourself. Not only will your baked goods scream with flavor and health, you'll love your new shapely grain-grinding muscular arms. I use a hand cranked "Country Living" grain mill that's almost identical to the one in this photo. A bit of flavor is lost as a result of the heat produced by an electric mill, but an electric mill is better than a poke in the face. My mill lives clamped to the kitchen counter and every time someone walks by it, they can't help but grind a bit of corn, wheat, or oats.

Photo courtesy of Library of Congress

Corn grinder in an Okla-homa farm field, 1939

Whole, unmilled grains are available mail-order and at your local green grocer or food co-op. But see what you can find close to home first. I'll bet there's someone growing heirloom corn, wheat or rye near you. If you don't grind your own grains, perhaps there's a nearby mill that does. There are hundreds of regional working grain mills in this country and a visit to an historic mill is a fun outing for the family. If you'd like to try your hand at baking and cooking with very fresh historic varieties of corn, wheat, rice, and ancient grains, then give Anson Mills, based in Charleston, South Carolina, a holler. They are grain-revivalists who work with local farmers to raise lost strains of corn, rice, buckwheat, oats and farro. You'll pay more for heritage varieties of grain than you would for its often genetically-modified sibling in a grocery store, but your taste buds as well as your conscience will thank you.

SPRING

A FARM WOMAN'S NOTES
Rural New Yorker, March 14, 1925

"For just as sure as the sap stirs in the aged roots of trees, and roots and seeds everywhere mysteriously swell and become alive, when Winter is apparently going it strong, so do we farmers feel deep within us the old dormant desire seething and stirring. Old Mother Nature is calling us along with her very own to be up and doing as good husbandmen should, to aid and abet her in bringing about the great Spring change."

Well put! This book begins with spring because that's when the growin' season begins. With life poking out of the ground any way it can, Spring is the season of planting and gathering. While recipes are abundant when it comes to the cooking of cultivated spring vegetables, we're just now getting back to our American and early immigrant roots as far as the gathering of spring's most special and tender treasures. Of course, we've been trying to get back to the old days of gathering for some time as evidenced by this writing in *American Cookery* magazine from May of 1919:

"Country children once were familiar with, and enjoyed the edible qualities of many native products, which today are scarcely known, since tropical fruits and manufactured sweets have found their way to the smallest village stores. The young wintergreen leaves, the artichokes, the sweet flag ground nuts, seeds of the sweet fern, and many others have been delights of country children from time immemorial. Almost anywhere along the highway or the railroad tracks, just now, we may see Italian women and those from other countries, who know the value of such foods better than many Americans, gathering the first dandelions for salads and greens."

You'll find lots of "weed" recipes in this chapter, some edible weeds you may recognize, and some you may need help in identifying. But one thing's for certain, you know what a dandelion is, and I'm just about positive you have them growing where you live.

MONTH OF MARCH

MARCH.

Weary are we of our winter-time fare;
Hasten, O Springtime, elusive and arch!
Bring us your dainties; our cupboards are bare!
Pity us, starved by tyrannical March!

March is the snarly 12 year-old you don't know whether to hug or holler at. Just when you've had enough of the same old starchy cold weather fare, here come sweet gifts born of the remnants of the soggy dregs of winter ... creasy greens (upland cress), forgotten tender scallions from last year's garden, and the tasty, obstinate offspring of dandelion wishes. Look down, supper's around here somewhere.

SPRING GREENS A BEAUTIFER
Economical Dishes for the Spring Season
Farm and Home, March 15, 1917

"It is well known that greens eaten freely in the spring tend to purify the blood and clear the complexion. There are a number of other garden greens, many of those usually classified as weeds, that

properly prepared make healthful as well as appetizing dishes. If we're so fortunate as to live in the country, we might find right in our own back yards, in fence corners, and in pasture fields many weeds that will make excellent greens for the table. Sorrel, lamb's quarters, milkweed, yellow curly dock, mustard leaves, nettle leaves, peppergrass, purslane, dandelion and many others we might name equally as good." (1917)

MONTH OF MARCH

DANDELION FLOWER SALAD
American Cookery, April 1918

"Dandelions make a delicious salad. Chop dandelions that have been gathered early in the morning while the dew is on them. They are tougher and stronger in taste after the sun has shone on them awhile. Just a dash of salt before serving and a sprinkle of cider vinegar. Very appetizing." (1918)

UNCOOKED DANDELION SALAD
Handwritten Recipe Book, 1918

"For this salad use the tender inside leaves of the dandelions, add a few tender lettuce leaves, a little sorrel and water cress. Wash and drain. Place in a dish lined with lettuce leaves, and pour over a French dressing. Serve while crisp and cool. A combination of dandelion leaves, cress or sorrel, and little balls of cottage cheese make a good salad. Serve with a French or mayonnaise dressing." (1918)

Author's note: French dressing would have been oil, vinegar, salt and pepper. If you have violets growing in your yard, toss some in.

"I have already stated my opinion on red onions. I do not want them. My markets almost reject them."

The New Onion Culture, 1903

MONTH OF MARCH

Cottage cheese is easy to make. All you need is skim milk, and something acid to set the curd; either buttermilk or vinegar. Or you can make a larger curd version using a mesophilic starter and rennet, available at cheesemaking shops, online, or your local organic market. (See resources, page 146.)

FRENCH COTTAGE CHEESE
Economy Cook Book, 1918

"Pour 1 quart of sour milk into an earthen mold which has holes in the bottom, or a very fine sieve may be used instead of the mold. The whey drips out and the curd assumes a custardlike consistency and takes the shape of the mold. When sufficiently stiff, the cheese is chilled, and is eaten with sweet cream and sugar. It is a staple dessert in many French families, especially in hot weather, and is delicious served with acid fruit, as currants, or strawberries." (1918)

TWO COTTAGE CHEESE GOODIES
Rural New-Yorker, March 3, 1923

"Cottage cheese should always be made from fresh clabber which has not been allowed to become too sour. Allow it to drip thoroughly, then mix well and season with good sweet cream, salt and pepper to taste, it should be eaten soon after making." (1923)

Cheese Balls with Jelly Sandwiches
"Spread lunch biscuits with raspberry jelly to form sandwiches along-side cottage cheese balls made from freshly-made cottage cheese well mixed and seasoned." (1923)

Cottage Cheese Sandwiches With Early Beets
"From your garden, gather the first spring beets while they are still tender and small, like big buttons. Cook and pour over them a rich, spicy vinegar. Let stand overnight and serve with milk biscuit and cottage cheese sandwiches. This makes a dainty appetizing lunch on early spring days." (1923)

MONTH OF MARCH

PORK CHOPS WITH BROWNED HOMINY
Mrs. Scott's North American Season Cook Book, 1921

For this recipe, use a cast iron skillet to cook your pork chops your favorite way. Though you can substitute canned Mexican hominy in this recipe, you'll prefer the flavor of dried hominy that's been soaked overnight and slow cooked for about 2 hours. See resources (page 146) for a source.

1 pound of pork chops
1 pound of hominy
Salt and pepper to taste

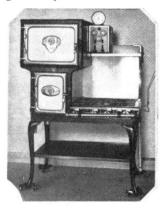

"Have small loin or rack chops cut five to the pound. Trim off the chine bone. Put the chops into a hot pan without fat. There's enough fat from the trimmings to fry the meat. Fry quickly, turning quite often. After the chops are browned nicely, season with salt and pepper. Place on the center of a platter. Put the hominy, which has been soaked overnight and boiled until tender (either in a fireless cooker or in front of cellar furnace) into pan after removing chops. Fry same as you would hashed browned potatoes. Season to taste, put around the chops and sprinkle with parsley." (1921)

Housekeeping Hints, 1888

If your griddle gets rough when you are frying batter cakes, take a raw turnip and slice off the end, and rub the griddle all over with it, and it will be as smooth as glass.

There is nothing better for cleaning steel knives than a raw Irish potato, dipped in fine brick dust. Cut off a slice of the potato so as to leave a raw surface, dip it in finely beaten brickdust, and rub the knives until they look bright and clean. It does not wear out and break the ends of the blades, and requires no strength at all.

Freshly fallen snow makes batter cakes as light as fresh laid eggs would do. Make up your batter as usual, only omitting the eggs, and when ready to commence baking them, take up lightly as many heaping tablespoonfuls of snow as you would have taken eggs and stir quickly into batter, and our experience is that the snow is as good as an egg.

MONTH OF MARCH

STORY OF THE WEALTHY APPLE
The Rural New-Yorker, March 3, 1923

Is this version of Peter Gideon's story true? I don't know. But there's been much written about this man whose horticultural efforts made it possible for apple trees to be grown in our cold northern climates. And for that, he's a hero. He named the apple after his wife, Wealthy. Now's the time to order and prepare a place for your apple trees if you didn't get them planted in the fall. I'm ordering a Wealthy apple tree for my garden today.

"About 1860 a pioneer at Excelsior, Minnesota, found himself in dire straits. The story runs that an invisible being appeared to him and told him to send his eight dollars to a certain address in Maine for apple seed. He had but one suit of clothes, and that was in wretched condition, but he took two vests and sewed them together to make a coat, and supplied sleeves to this makeshift garment by cutting off the legs from an old pair of trousers. In lieu of shoes, he swathed his feet in gunny sacks. And so this perservering horticulturist planted with faith the seed of the Cherry Crab that he purchased from Maine with the last of the wealth he possessed. The world has ever sung the praises of Peter M. Gideon, the originator of a famous apple, for from one of these seeds sprang the tree destined to be named "Wealthy." It's the queen of the king of fruits." (1923)

TO DESTROY INSECTS PREJUDICIAL TO APPLE-TREES
The Household Receipt Book, 1853

"To one hundred gallons of human urine, and one bushel of lime, add cow-dung to bring it to the consistency of paint. With this composition anoint the trees. The month of March is the proper season for applying it." (1853)

Author's note: Sorry! This was just too stinky to pass up.

MONTH OF MARCH

It ain't no use puttin' up yer umbrell' till it rains.

BAKED APPLES WITH OATMEAL
Housekeeper's Apple Book, 1918

"Core apples; fill the space from which the core was taken with cold cooked oatmeal. Stand the apples in a baking dish, sprinkle with sugar, and add half a cup of water. Bake in a moderate oven until soft. Serve with cream, using a little more oatmeal for garnish." (1918)

Courtesy Library of Congress

THE MAGAZINE FARMER
People's Home Journal, March 1907

I used to like the old place, but now it ain't no use;
It's laid out inartistic, and it's tacky as the deuce;
You see I've been a-reading, till envy makes me green,
Of artistic agriculture in a farming magazine.

It tells you how your pig pen should be on aesthetic lines;
And your Looey Fourteen henhouse should be draped in ivy vines;
I'm goin' to sell the old place-It's architecture's bum,
And I'll buy one of them dream joints, in that magazine, by gum!

I'll raise no crops plebeian, but I'll put in plants and shrubs;
I'll do no harvest sweatin', leave that fer the old time dubs!
I may not last a season, 'fore I meet the sheriff man,
But I'm goin to be a farmer on the magazinist plan!

MONTH OF
M A R C H

POPOVERS
Things Mother Used to Make, 1913

Perhaps Lydia Maria Gurney has gone a bit too far with her "collection of old-time recipes, some nearly 100 years old that are written very plainly, for those who have had no experience, no practice and possibly have little judgement." Excuse me?? I have plenty of judgement, I just don't have anything to measure my flour with! But back to popovers, a fun old, old, old food that's worth a few trials to get right. By the way, Ms. Gurney's book really is good, but I'm amending her recipe because her popovers don't pop as high as mine. Ha!

Dumped a cup of flour into it.

1 Egg	**1 Cupful of Milk**
1 Cupful of Flour	**A little salt**

"Beat the egg, and stir flour and milk in slowly, a little flour, then a little milk. Salt a little. This will make a very thin batter. Drop into well-buttered muffin pan, bake in a very hot oven and serve with butter." (1913)

Author's note: Popover-making takes practice. Altitude, flour, size of eggs all affect outcome. All in all, fallen popovers are almost as good as puffy ones!

1 cup milk	**1 Tbs. melted butter**
½ tsp. salt	**2 eggs**
1 cup flour	

Whisk together milk, salt, butter, and eggs. Stir in flour until barely blended. Fill popover pan or buttered muffin cups halfway full. Put pan into cold oven, turn it on to 450º. After 15 minutes, turn oven to 350º and bake 20 minutes or until golden and crunchy. Don't open oven until you check to see if they're done. Punch hole in each as they come out of the oven to release steam. Another method is to preheat oven to 450º, heat pan, then grease and add batter. Bake for 15 minutes, then turn oven to 350º and bake for 15 or 20 more minutes. Add a little water to unused muffin pan holes before baking.

MONTH OF
MARCH

CARROT CONSERVE
Prepare! 1918

"The children will enjoy this on their bread or cakes. It is easily made and inexpensive. Select young carrots, scrape and wash them, then slice thin. Cover with cold water and cook till soft enough to press through a sieve. Measure the pulp and add the strained juice of two lemons, and the grated rind of one lemon and one orange, also three-fourths of the quantity of light brown sugar. Cook till thick, and pour into tumblers." (1918)

Author's note: To 1 lb. carrots, use juice and rind of 1 lemon, and rind of half an orange. Give softened carrots a whirl in food processor or run through a food mill. Measure pulp and follow directions as written. Tasty on cornmeal waffles.

GRAPEFRUIT SORBET
I Go A-Marketing, 1900

"If you want a grapefruit sorbet, you may pick out the pulp with a fork in sizable bits, free from seeds and pith, cover these bits with sherry and with a sprinkling of sugar and freeze. You know the rest — how to serve it and the like." (1900)

Author's note: Just in case you don't know the rest, you can try this:

½ cup sugar	3 really good red grapefruits & 1 tsp. zest
¼ cup water	1 Tbs. vodka (helps with texture)

Make a sugar syrup by barely simmering sugar in water just until the sugar dissolves. Chill. Remove about a teaspoon of zest from a grapefruit. Now halve grapefruits and juice, keeping the shell in good shape. Combine zest, juice, vodka or sherry and syrup to taste, then pour into your ice cream machine and freeze. Serve in empty grapefruit halves (you'll want to remove the leftover pulp first). Garnish with some shreds of dried cranberry or fresh mint if available.

MONTH OF MARCH

NOVELTY DESSERT
1930's Handwritten Cookbook

While this recipe isn't all that exciting, the story behind the words is. It comes from a handwritten cookbook I just bought online; I love unraveling the mysteries behind such gems. The recipes are from acquaintances of the author and late 19th century ladies magazines like Hearth and Home, Ladies World, Comfort, Happy Hours and Housewife. The handwriting is lovely, but what I love most are the references to period kitchenware that women had in their homes during this era like an agate saucepan, earthenware pudding dish and flat iron. The directive to move the fruit to the back of the range suggests a wood or coal oven that would have kept a fire throughout the day. Anyhow, if you have a stale cake lying around, a quart jar of last years' blackberries, a Guernsey cow that produces thick, rich cream, and a flat iron, here's something you can whip up for dinner.

"A freshly baked cottage pudding or some stale cake may be the foundation for this dessert. Open a quart jar of blackberries. Pour into an agate saucepan and bring to the boiling point. Move it to the back of the range to keep warm till wanted. Place squares of the cake in an earthenware pudding dish, cover with generous spoonfuls of the hot berries and juice, then another layer of cake and packing it well, then add more berries. Repeat until the dish is full using plenty of juice. Cover with a plate and place flat iron on. When cool, take out, and slice evenly. Serve with thick rich cream." (1930s)

MONTH OF
M A R C H

MAPLE POP-CORN
Mrs. Allen's Cook Book, 1917

"3 quarts popped corn, 1 cupful maple syrup, ½ cupful granulated sugar. Boil the syrup and sugar together until it spins a thread. Pour onto corn, stir well, cool." (1917)

Author's note: This is GREAT! Pop ½ cup popcorn kernels. Boil ½ cup maple syrup, ¼ sugar, 2 Tbs. butter to 240º, and then stir in a pinch of baking soda. Add a light sprinkling of salt after mixing syrup with the corn. For Cracker Jack, substitute molasses for the maple syrup. If soggy, bake 15 minutes at 250º.

CRACKER JACK
How to do Things, 1919

"One cupful of brown sugar, one cupful extracted honey or sorghum. Boil until it hardens when dropped into cold water. Remove from the fire and stir in one-fourth teaspoonful of soda, and when this is dissolved, stir in all the popcorn it will take. Spread on greased tins and mark into squares." (1919)

In 1922, Rueckheim Bros. & Eckstein changed their name to " The Cracker Jack Company" because only an infinitesimal percentage of the people who bought and ate Cracker Jack had any idea who made it. Neither did they care.

POP CORN BALLS (VERY OLD RECIPE)
Things Mother Used to Make, 1913

"Boil together 1 cupful of molasses and a piece of butter half the size of an egg until it strings (240º), and then stir in a pinch of soda. Put this over a quart dish full of popped corn. When cool enough to handle, squeeze into balls the size of an orange." (1913)

Author's note: Careful with this one, the molasses burns very quickly.

MONTH OF APRIL

What a lively month in the kitchen garden! Asparagus, peppery and pungent watercress, creasy greens, rocket, radishes, little early salad fixin's, spinach, slim and tender green onions, morel mushrooms, the beginnings of rhubarb. And then there's the end of last year's preserved harvest that needs to be consumed to make room in the pantry for this summer's bounty.

Trout season opens here in the western North Carolina mountains in early April. That would be the time that my husband, Wayne, heads to the nearby stream with his father's pole and threadbare creel and comes back with rainbow trout that I stuff with thyme and rosemary and bind with a piece of bacon to sizzle over a waiting campfire. Or not. Sometimes we have grilled veggies for dinner instead, if you know what I mean.

April
Tell me, housewife blithe and fair
How does your garden grow!
Crisp and green the lettuce there,
Onions, row by row.

EMBER BROILED TROUT
Mother's Cook Book, 1902

If the above recipe doesn't suit you, try this. Dip the trout in egg whites and then dredge in flour or cornmeal. Cast iron pan-fry in a little butter.

"Clean and split them open, season with a little salt and cayenne; dip in whipped egg, dredge with flour and brander over a clear fire." (1902)

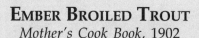

Brander: To broil or cook on an iron trivet or gridiron over live fire or embers. In 1902, the fish probably was "brandered" in a skillet over a trivet as the coating would have stuck to the bars of this version of an 1846 gridiron.

MONTH OF APRIL

"Gather sorrel early in the morning, wash thoroughly; chop two cups of sorrel in a bowl with one-half cup of seeded raisins and one-half cup of nuts; walnuts are fine if you were fortunate enough to gather some last fall; add French or mayonnaise dressing and serve garnished with sorrel." (1918)

Author's note: Any pungent spring greens will do, like arugula, cress, or dandelion greens. Top with rhubarb vinaigrette and toasted walnuts or almonds.

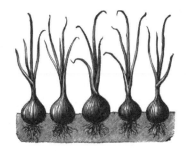

RHUBARB VINAIGRETTE

The rule of thumb for a vinaigrette is three parts olive oil to one of vinegar. The rhubarb syrup takes the sour edge off the vinegar, but it's very sweet. Start with just a little and then add more to your liking. Leftover syrup makes a tasty chicken glaze or try a little mixed with seltzer and fresh lemon juice.

1 tsp. shallots, chopped	Rhubarb syrup to taste
2 Tbs. red wine vinegar	3-6 Tbs. olive oil or walnut oil
Pinch Dijon mustard	Salt and pepper to taste

Combine shallots, vinegar, mustard, rhubarb syrup, salt and pepper and gradually whisk in oil.

Rhubarb Syrup: Combine 1 cup chopped rhubarb, 1/4 cup sugar and 1/4 cup water. Simmer 10 or so minutes till thick. Strain (eat the rhubarb sauce strainings!)

"Onions are a good tonic for the nerves, so it will pay to lay in a good supply this winter. Parsnips also have a medicinal value, according to scientists, who claim that they possess the same virtues that sarsaparilla does.
Woman's Farm Journal, 1906

MONTH OF
A P R I L

DANDELION BLOSSOM HONEY

Our Czech friends Martin & Denisa Zak live in the forest outside a small village north of Prague. On a recent visit one chilly October morning, they served dandelion honey atop a warm slice of Denisa's fabulous homemade rye bread that she had baked in their antique tile wood cookstove made by Martin. This syrup looks EXACTLY like honey, but has a faint floral springtime flavor. Here is the recipe in Martin's words:

Denisa cooking dinner

"This is a traditional recipe passed down from the old-world Europeans. I use it as a substitute for honey in any recipe that I'm trying to make wild."

> **4 cups dandelion flowers (pluck yellow flowers from stem)**
> **4 cups water   4 cups sugar**
> **1 organic lemon or orange sliced, peel and all**

The citrus is optional, it will give the syrup an orangey or lemony flavor. If you want the pure dandelion flavor, you can skip the citrus. I make it both ways each year.

1. Put petals from about 400 blossoms, water and lemon in a pot.
2. Bring just to a boil, turn off heat, cover, and let sit overnight.
3. The next day, strain and press liquid out of spent flowers.
4. Add sugar and heat slowly, stirring now and again, for several hours or until reduced to a thick, honey-like syrup. (Keep it just under a simmer or it will caramelize.)
5. Can in half-pint jars.

"This recipe makes a little more than 1 pint. I usually triple or quadruple this, and I make more than one batch when the blossoms are in season to have enough for the year. The syrup makes great Christmas presents, so make plenty!"

MONTH OF
A P R I L

CURLED GARDEN CRESS SALAD
Unfired Foods, 1912

"Lay a bunch of cress on a chopping board and cut off thin slices, thus mincing it. Mix into this, an equal weight of cocoanut grated, peanuts, pignolias flaked or other nuts chopped. You can add a teaspoonful each of honey and olive oil. Mix these till the cress is dressed." (1912)

This recipe is from my new favorite book, *Unfired Foods*. Smack dab in the middle of a turn-of-the-century raw, vegan, vegetarian food rebellion, the book boasts "360 Recipes for health drinks, uncooked soups, fruit, flower and vegetable salads, unbaked breads and brawn foods."

While I can't disagree with the author's advice "to eat natural food to maintain and increase your physical and spiritual health and avoid all food which ensnares the appetite with artificial flavors and chemically changed consistency," I do wonder about this advertisement at the end of the book for Mother's X-Ray Curing Lamp for baby.

MOTHER'S X-RAY CURING LAMP

Alarmed by the possibility that actual X-ray machines might have been available for home use in 1912, I consulted with a radiation historian, an expert on antique lighting, and my medical physicist daughter, Annie, to find out more. To my great relief, "mother" was not actually irradiating her baby's back-side. According to Tim Tromp of bulbcollector.com, "Quack comes to mind when viewing this ad. The word, X-ray was new during the early 1900s and many companies exploited the term to generate excitement for their products. This is just an incandescent lamp fixture and nothing more." Paul Frame, Radiation Historian at URAU (Oak Ridge Associated Universities) agrees, "The term X-ray was somewhat magical and it was attached to all sorts of brand names."

MONTH OF
A P R I L

Pretty much, eating cooked foods makes you a total loser. Since I, my-self, am such a loser, I'll just turn you over to George J. Drews to make his convincing case as he did in his 1912 book, Unfired Foods. He's got himself all worked up on the subject, so I'm giving him two pages to get all this off his chest.

"Some people are so perversely civi-lized, so would be aristocratic, so imagi-narily refined, so goody-goody mannered and so ridiculously delicate and dainty-mouthed that they dare not, and often cannot, eat natural foods; that natural foods choke them and that, even their ig-norantly trained stomach revolts against natural foods. In this perversity, however, they are perfectly willing to be a fashionable sarcophag or necrop-hag (carrion eater). They are proud to be fashionably sick and pay a fashionable doctor and they have the wonderful courage to swallow the customary, most nauseating drugs irrespective of the dangerous after effects the expected cure may lead to."

Youth Obtaind & Retaind
George White, MD, 1921

Like the spelling? Dr. White was a supporter of the Simpli-fied Spelling Movement of 1905, whose goal was to increase literacy among English-speakers. The simplified spellers and the unfired food eaters were both part of the same early 20th century artsy, bohemian, nonconformist, freethinking urban American scene.

Eat only one-fifth as much as yu think yu need.

Exercize regularly and sistematically.

Be happy that yu don't hav so much trubl as sum other fello.

As much as possibl, adhere to a raw diet.

Do not eat mushes, unnatural sweets, meat, glucose or saccharin.

Do not be afraid of catching any diseas. Fear is the worst dis-eas of all.

MONTH OF APRIL

"When the house is provided, and the woman who has dreamed of a true home is settled therein, it gradually dawns upon her that instead of being a queen, she is an imprisoned vassal. She finds that she must stand over a miniature furnace for an hour in the morning and breathe the poisonous odor of broiling flesh, and spend another hour among the grease and slime of pots and dishes, instead of occupying that time walking in the life-giving sunlight and drinking in nature's purifying air."

Courtesy Library of Congress, 1914

> ### WOMAN
> *"Queen of the Home" say the Anti-Suffragists*
> *Yes; Queen of a Cook-Stove Throne*

"She soon realizes that the fires of the morning are hardly out until those for the noon are kindled and the labors from luncheon often lap over into the evening, and those of evening far into the night. The throne over which she dreamed of wielding the queenly sceptre has been transformed into a fiery furnace, gilded with greasy pots and plates, blood and bones, over which she has unfurled the dishrag, and by the common custom of her country, it waves over her helpless head as a sign of her rank and profession, under which she is really a slave."

Unfired Foods, 1912

Observe the Turnip in the pot,
The Tern is glad that he is not!

MONTH OF APRIL

It's a bird, it's a plane, No! It's asparagus! Superheroes of spring, they fly through rich, loamy soil ready to rescue us from a barren, forlorn winter larder. If you don't grow asparagus at your place, you must go visit someone who does; they are an astonishing piece of work, the way they assert themselves for the plucking. The sweet early purple stalks don't make it much past their nest in my garden, asparagus is sweetest when freshly snapped. As with all the best seasonal foods, when they're in, they're in like crazy ... and when they're gone, they're not worth eating.

A Sparrer. Asparagus.

The Sparrow, from flying, is quite
out of breath,
In fact he has worked himself
almost to death,
While the lazy Asparagus, —
—so it is said,—
Spends all of his time in the
'sparagus bed.

MARINATED ASPARAGUS SALAD

Cook asparagus just a few minutes until tender. Plunge into cold water and then toss with a vinaigrette made from olive oil, fresh lemon juice, garlic, chili flakes, salt and pepper. Refrigerate a couple hours, then thread through a couple purple onion rings and serve atop fresh spring greens.

ASPARAGUS IN AMBUSH
Gold Medal Flour Cook Book, 1910

2 bunches cooked asparagus
1 cup milk
2 eggs
1 tablespoon butter

1 tablespoon Gold Medal flour
¼ tsp. salt
Pinch pepper
6 rolls

"Cut off the tops of the rolls to serve as covers. Remove the crumb, dust the shells and covers with melted butter and brown in the oven. Make a white sauce of the milk, butter and flour. Cut the tender part of the asparagus fine, cook a few minutes in the white sauce; fill the rolls with the mixture, place on the tops and serve hot." (1910)

Author's note: Hey, what happened to the eggs? You can add or omit them.

MONTH OF
A P R I L

MY NEIGHBOR'S CHICKS
Rural New Yorker, March 14, 1925

Why is it that my neighbor's flock is laying every day?
He hasn't any better stock but how his hens do lay!
While I have trouble with my brood,
                they are dying by the score,
His chickens quickly eat their food
                and then they lay some more.
While I can hardly meet my bills, my notes are due tomorrow,
His limosine climbs up the hills, he hasn't any sorrow!
The truth about this story is: the one who's failing in his biz,
Whose chickens die, or are so sick ...
           Has not been feeding Diamond Pick!

HOW TO SAVE EGGS
Good Housekeeping, April, 1889

—Pack eggs in layers, small end down, in bran, corn meal, saw dust or oats. The bran and oats are the least liable to gather moisture.

—Wrap each egg in paper (news paper will do) as oranges are in their crates, then pack in layers. Take care there is no break in the paper or slackness in the twisted ends and the eggs will keep three months.

—Cover each egg with a coating of a mixture of beeswax and olive or cotton-seed oil; using one-third wax to two-thirds oil.

MONTH OF APRIL

COCOA "ANGLE" CAKE
McNess Cook Book, 1920

ndeed, isn't this a fascinating cake, spelling aside. It's an unsophisticated angel food cake that takes only five minutes to prepare. Try it with fresh strawberries; it's good if you don't mind the carcinogenic flavoring. Curious about cumarin (sic) in food, I consulted the 1919 "Simmons Spice Mill," a coffee, tea, and spice trade magazine. Turns out coumarin, derived from tonka beans, has a flavor similar to vanilla and was added to imitation vanilla to enhance the flavor. It's been banned for use in food products in America due to its toxicity to liver, kidneys and lungs. Always bake with real vanilla.

"Whites 5 eggs, ½ teaspoon cream tartar, beat until dry; add gradually 1 cup granulated sugar with which ¼ cup of F.W. McNess's Breakfast Cocoa has been sifted; ½ teaspoon McNess' Vanilla, Vanillin and cumarin, fold in carefully ½ cup flour; bake in tube pan ½ hour 350º."

LEMON ANGEL PIE

Speaking of angel cake, here's another handy angel dessert that can be used as a "pie crust" to hold any fresh fruit that comes into season all summer. This meringue is from a 1930s handwritten recipe card. The filling is a lemon curd minus the butter. I'd add a couple tablespoons of butter to the mixture when you add the lemon juice.

3 egg whites	**3 egg yolks**
¾ tsp. cream of tartar	**½ cup sugar**
¾ cup sugar	**Juice and rind of 2 lemons**

"Add cream of tartar to egg whites and beat until stiff, but not dry. Gradually add 1 cup sugar and continue beating until stiff and glossy. Spread in a greased pie plate and bake at 275º for 40 minutes until only slightly browned. Meanwhile, beat egg yolks with sugar and then add lemon juice and rind and cook in double boiler until a spoon leaves a trail. Cool. Whip 1 cup cream and spread half on cooled meringue. Cover with lemon filling and top with remaining cream and a sprinkle of rind. Chill." (1930s)

MONTH OF APRIL

(CURRANT-CARAWAY) SODA CAKES

365 Cakes and Cookies, 1904

If it's April 3rd, we must be having currant caraway soda cakes for dessert. I know this because that's what my trusty 365 Cakes and Cookies book tells me. Written by "pinkies-up" domestic economy ladies for housewives who cook, the recipes are truly seasonal, and this month we're stuck with dried fruit since our root-cellared apples are all gone and the strawberries aren't in yet.

Soda Cakes.

Mix 1 teaspoonful of baking soda with 1 pound of flour and rub into it ½ pound of warmed butter. When quite smooth, add 3 well-beaten eggs, ½ pound of cleaned currants, ½ pound of sugar, and a few caraway seeds. Mix well and bake in small tins.

CARAWAY

Down past the savory-bed and the parsley,
  And close to the tumble-down picket-fence,
The caraway grew that Grandma planted,
  And there it has been growing ever since.

 ## HOME IDEAS and ⸘ECONOMIES⸘

Do not waste anything in the kitchen. Our grandmothers scrupulously saved every piece of bone or fat, and these were utilized in making soft soap.

The careful housekeeper will manage to keep out of debt and set a good table, with much variety, on a small allowance, by faithfully saving and utilizing the left-overs.

Never throw away any beet, turnip or radish tops. They may all be cooked in the same manner as spinach au jus, or they may be boiled with salt meat, and make very good and healthful dishes.

~ The Picayune Creole Cook Book, 1922

MONTH OF MAY

retty May days are like spring-scented, clothesline dried, crisp cotton sheets on the just-made bed that's covered with a hand stitched yellow-flowered quilt. The New Year may be a time for taking stock of ourselves, but May is when we take charge. We're gripped with tidy ambitiousness inside and out. Windows washed, floors scrubbed, flower beds mulched. The kitchen garden sprouts cheerful rows of lettuce, greens, radishes, beets, chard, herbs, spring onions and strawberries, all ready to pick for supper. Summer vegetables and fruits are planted and growing and a calm descends as we admire our completely young and weedless work of art.

To Woman on the Witness Stand

Sovereign Woman vs. Mere Man, 1905

"Please tell the Court what you did between eight and nine o'clock on that morning."

"I gave the two children their breakfast, dressed them for school, made up their lunches, washed the dishes, made the beds, sorted the soiled linen and put it in the tubs, swept and dusted the parlor, sewed a button or two on the children's clothes, interviewed the gas man, grocer, and butcher, put off the landlord, sat down to glance over the morning paper, and then ..."

"That will do madam."

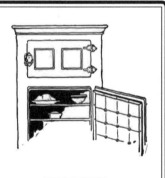

ICE BOX RULE

Keep your ice box clean and neat,
For it holds the things you eat;
Milk and butter, to be nice,
Must be kept against the ice;
As they quickly spoil and smell,
You must have them covered well;
Fruit and vegetables should go
With the meat, on shelves below.

~*When Mother Let's Us Help,*
1916

MONTH OF M A Y

MAY.

Scrub and polish,—sweep and clean,——
  Fling your windows wide!
See, the trees are clad in green!
  Coax the spring inside!
Home, be shining fair to-day
For the guest whose name is May!

~*How to Please a Husband*, 1917

On the other hand, maybe we're not having so much fun ...

If women, especially farm women, had for housekeeping, appliances as up-to-date as their husbands have for their businesses, health-destroying drudgery from early till late would be unnecessary. Small wonder now that "woman's work is never done."
~*Good Housekeeping*, December, 1916

Mrs. Kemp's "Pasteys"
Michigan Women's Superior Cook Book, 1905

"2 quarts of Dousman's Best Patent flour, one pound of lard, one-half teaspoon of salt. Rub well together and wet with cold water as you mix pie-crust. Roll out in sheets the size of a tea-plate and then place on one-half of the dough, sliced potatoes, then porterhouse steak cut in small pieces, pepper, salt and a little onion. Two pounds of porterhouse steak and the above amount of crust will make six pasteys. For those who like turnip, use turnips sliced in with the potatoes." (1905)

Here's where I confess that I'm allergic to beef and so I can't tell you about this pasty or any other. But my friend Pam can, and she shared with me her recipe that's been in the family for generations. She entered her pasty in our pie contest recently and it disappeared in seconds. Speaking of contests, don't miss the annual summer Pastyfest held in Calumet, Michigan. Games, a parade and a pasty bake-off celebrate the pie that immigrated to the Calumet community from Europe in the 1880s.

It's said that pastys originated in Cornwall, England and were brought with Finnish miners to the Upper Peninsula of Michigan in the 19th century. Pam says, "My mother told me that women made these for their husbands for lunch. The men would come out of the mines and have fresh pastys to eat." A short pie crust made from lard and suet is traditional, but feel free to use your own recipe. (I doubt you'll like Mrs. Kemp's crust recipe.)

Pam's Pasty

Pam's Pastys

1 cup raw potatoes, cubed
1 cup raw rump roast, cubed
½ cup onions, chopped
½ tsp. salt (or to your taste)
Pepper

Makes one big pasty. Combine ingredients and place off-center on your dough. Fold and crimp edges as in photo. Bake at 400º 1 hour.

MONTH OF
M A Y

Grow your own

BEET GREENS
Us Two Cook Book, 1909

"Wash carefully the leaves and stalks of young beets. Boil until tender in an uncovered vessel. Drain and season with butter. Beet greens are very nice served with corn beef hash." (1909)

FRESH PEAS WITH PEARL ONIONS AND BACON

Shell as many fresh peas as you need for dinner. Blanch in boiling water a couple of minutes. Fish the peas out of the blanching water, then boil a handful of pearl onions for 5 minutes. Slip the skins off. Fry a couple slices of lean bacon in a cast iron skillet. Drain the fat, throw your peeled onions into the pan and cook until the onions are lightly caramelized. Add the peas, crumbled bacon and salt and pepper to taste.

WHEN MOTHER LETS US COOK

Of Shoe-soles and Corks, 1929

If you are fond of walking you will find the shoes you use for this purpose will last longer if the soles are dipped into melted wax every few weeks. This will also make them waterproof.

When the time has come to put up catsup, you wonder why you threw away all those corks. Start a box right now and keep corks and pieces of paraffin from jellies in it, and you will be very grateful in preserving time.

~Hagerstown Town and Country Almanack

MONTH OF
M A Y

I Go A-Marketing, 1900

I am in love with Henrietta Sowle's seasonal farm-market book, "I Go A-Marketing." Published in 1900, it's a running chat with the housekeeper or housewife about what's good at the market on any given month of the year and all the fun things you can do with your produce. Evidently, May is the month when you should eat veal. In fact, she has your whole dinner figured out for you. The veal follows olives stuffed with caviar, creamed pea and spinach soup, fresh pineapple, maybe some ember-baked potatoes, a few asparagus tops broiled with cheese, and is followed by a rhubarb sorbet. What the heck, I'll just include her whole meal for you!

Pea and Spinach Soup

"Now, for a soup. Soak overnight a pint of green dried peas. Drain, and cook in plenty of fresh water till perfectly tender. Then press through a sieve. Have cooked, at the same time, a peck of spinach, and press through a sieve also. Then put the two purées together, season with salt and pepper; heat well, adding half a pint of milk. Just before taking up, pour in a pint of cream, and serve with tiny squares of fried bread in the tureen. Ever heard of this before? It's a soup that is rich and delicate, but not so hearty that it does more than whet the appetite for what is to follow." (1900)

Author's note: Forget the sieve, just add a handful of greens to however many fresh or split peas you want to cook and purée the mixture. Cream is optional.

Asparagus Tops With Cheese

"Cut the tender part of the asparagus into inch-lengths and cook in salted water till fairly tender; then drain and toss about over the fire in a frying-pan with a little butter. Dress it on a vegetable dish, spread the surface smoothly with butter into which has been kneaded an equal quantity of grated Parmesan cheese and just a suspicion of cayenne pepper. Brown as quickly as you can in a piping hot oven, and serve." (1900)

I Go A-Marketing, continued ...

BROILED VEAL CUTLETS

"But if, some fine morning, a breath of winter comes o'er the land, via an east wind, then you will, perhaps, crave food served hot, in which case have veal cutlets (veal is in fine shape now). Dip them in melted butter and then broil over the coals; you will find this an infinitely better way of cooking them than by frying, which so many housekeepers consider the standard method. Or, if you do not care for veal, try thin slices of bacon, broiled, and served on toasted graham bread." (1900)

FRESH PINEAPPLE

"As a fruit, for leading up to either of these dishes, I think you will prefer pineapples, for they are of delicious quality now, and sold at a price which also recommends them to your notice." (Henrietta recommends you douse the pineapple with a bit of orange liqueur.)

RHUBARB SHERBET (SORBET)

In case you're curious, the liquid carmine called for in this recipe comes from cochineal, an insect that hangs out on certain cacti from which is extracted carminic acid that's used to make red carmine dye. Yummy. A red Bordeaux or other light red wine can pass for the claret. Last fall's frozen muscadine or other grape juice goes well with this sorbet in place of some or all of the claret. Just increase the lemon juice and sweeten lightly so that the rhubarb stays tart. Oh, and forget the carmine or other red dye.

"For dessert, why not a rhubarb sherbet? Cut up two pounds of it, and boil with a few drops of water and plenty of sugar, the rind of a lemon, and a little liquid carmine to color it prettily. Let this get cool; strain through a sieve, and add to it a pint of claret and two tablespoonfuls of rum. Freeze, and have ready to decorate it, when serving, some strips of candied ginger." (1900)

MONTH OF M A Y

Mrs. P.D.'s Chocolate Pudding
Practical Recipes, 1909

Somewhere between a Victorian-era steamed pudding and a cake baked in a tube pan, the hole in a chocolate cake like this one is a perfect place to park fresh-picked strawberries. The grated chocolate is a winner.

1 large cup of grated unsweetened Baker's chocolate

1 small cup of flour	**2 eggs well beaten**
1 large cup pulverized sugar	**½ cup of milk**
1 small cup of butter	**1 teaspoon soda**

To be baked in a mould with hole in center like old-fashioned cake pans. Fill center with freshly whipped cream." (1909)

Author's note: Try this: Grate two squares unsweetened chocolate using large holes of a box grater and set aside. Cream 6 Tbs. unsalted butter with 1 cup sugar. Beat in 2 eggs, one at a time. Add 1 tsp. vanilla. Sift ¾ cup flour with ½ tsp. baking powder, ½ tsp. baking soda and ¼ tsp. salt. Add alternately to creamed mixture with ½ cup milk. Pour into buttered tube pan. There are some great decorative cake pans available in kitchen stores and online. (See resources, page 146) Bake the cake at 350º until springy and lightly browned.

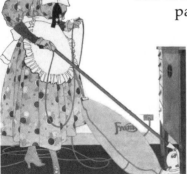

Cleaning With Rhubarb
Farm and Home Magazine, 1917

Put aluminum ware in a big pan and add a few stalks of rhubarb. Fill up with water and let come to a boil. This will clean and brighten the ware without injuring it.
Author's warning: Don't eat the rhubarb! (It reacts with the aluminum.)

MONTH OF M A Y

STRAWBERRY BIRDNEST FOR THE INVALID
Needlework Guild Cook Book, 1906

After the jams and jellies section of all pre-depression-era cookbooks, you'll find a selection of recipes "for the invalid." It fell upon the home cook, a.k.a. Mother, to tend to the sick members of the family. All manner of frightening miseries laid us low back then ... whooping cough, diphtheria, measles, mumps, chicken pox. The Spanish influenza of 1918 was a global disaster that infected one in four Americans. We were a sick bunch. If someone you love falls ill during strawberry season, here's what to serve; even if all's well, you'll find this dish as comforting as a gentle head rub.

1 cupful rice	**¼ teaspoonful salt**
2 cupfuls milk	**1 quart strawberries**

"Pick over rice, wash in several waters and put with milk and salt in double boiler. Cook until milk is absorbed and rice is tender. Make a nest of the rice, put strawberries in the nest and around it, and serve with cream and sugar."

Author's note: You don't need to fuss over the rice. Just cook as usual with water, adding a little milk at the end to soften it enough to stick together to make your nests. Short grain rices are stickier.

SATURDAY, JUNE 2.

Mock Lemon Pie (Very Good).
Bake in two crusts one cupful of chopped rhubarb, one egg, one cupful of sugar, one rolled cracker, and butter the size of a walnut.

Good Housekeeping 1888

MONTH OF
M A Y

1894 ... "I have accidentally come across a recipe for "sun-cooked" strawberry preserves, for which I had been inquiring for many years. I had a child's vivid recollection of a jar of most delicious strawberry preserves, that were given to my grandmother. Never since then have I tasted anything like them until I tried the following recipe, and since then every one who has tasted mine says they have more of the fresh fruit flavor than any they ever tasted."

"If possible, gather the fruit when dry, cap and weigh, and add equal weight of granulated sugar. Let sugar and berries stand together until some sirup has formed, then set on a stove (and, by the by, have an oil stove for preserving, as being labor saving and heat saving), let come to a boil and boil quite steadily for ten minutes, then dip out into dishes and set in the sun until the sirup becomes almost jelly-like in thickness. From sixteen to twenty hours of bright, hot sunshine should be enough. One cannot always get this much, though, in two days, as at this season rains and clouds are frequent. The sirup will thicken just left on the shallow dishes and set in a dry room."

"When thick enough put in small jars about pint size and seal tight. This is not absolutely necessary, but everything keeps better with air excluded. Jelly glasses may be used very well, made air-tight by pasting on fold after fold of tissue paper smeared with flour paste. Press this down smoothly and firmly, squeezing out all bubbles or wrinkles, and it can be made absolutely air-tight. Cooking will take all the color out of the berries, so just before taking them off the stove add enough pokeberry jelly or some fruit coloring to make any color desired; they are far prettier, and appearances go a long way in making things taste better." **(Warning ... Pokeberries are toxic.)**

Sun-cooked Strawberry Preserves, continued ...

"Don't put in tinware in the sun, but any kind of earthen or glassware will answer. Flies, bees and insects of all sorts would swarm about if not covered over, and frames covered over with wire gauze netting will serve every purpose. Mosquito netting will do if the wire cannot be obtained." (1894)

STRAWBERRY-MINT PRESERVES

Get ready to be ruined for life. One taste of this jam drizzled on an oatcake topped with local goat chevre and you will be rendered speechless. A bit fussier than the pectin-added method, but infinitely better. You'll need a candy thermometer and small kitchen scale to make jams by this method.

For every pound of fresh strawberries, you will need about 12 oz. white sugar and ½ of a juicy lemon. Cut the tops off the berries, and let macerate in sugar and lemon juice an hour or so. Bring to a boil and stir until sugar is dissolved. Remove from heat and cool, pour into a ceramic bowl and let sit in the refrigerator overnight covered with a plate. Next day, strain off the liquid and boil until it reaches 220º. Add the berries and return to 220º. Add about 10 chopped mint leaves and then follow rec-

ommendations for water-bath canning. (See resources for suggested reading, page 146) Makes about 5 half-pint jars.

Hints: I know you're tempted to decrease the sugar, but don't! There's an art to being able to tell when your jam has set. Stick a plate in the freezer and drizzle a little of the syrup onto the cold surface. Swipe your finger through the syrup; if it stays put on either side of the "swipe," then it's set. Better to undercook than overcook your fruit. It's fine if your preserves are a little runny.

SUMMER

t's summer and you're expecting to read something about all the hot-weather veggies you can pick or buy from your local farmers. We'll get to that, but first I want to talk about cordial making. If you are inclined to indulge in a nip here and there, fruit-flavored cordials and bounces are a lovely way to capture the fleeting essence of summer. They make great gifts. Just when winter gift-giving season arrives, your little fruity darlings will be ready to sample. I package mine in eight ounce decorative corked bottles sporting labels with colorful vintage graphics, along with a variety of teensy cordial glasses scavenged at thrift shops.

Big Scary Tin Man
Blackberry Bounce
It'll put your gut on fire.
Contains:
Blackberries, vodka, sugar.

A cordial contains fruit, sugar, and vodka. A bounce is made with brandy or whiskey. You can use any fruit in season, they're all dandy. I make strawberry, cherry, blueberry, black raspberry (the king of cordials), blackberry, peach, plum, red raspberry, currant, elderberry, pear, and cranberry. Use 100 proof vodka to insure that your cordials will not spoil at room temperature. Most of my bounces contain both brandy and vodka for this reason. Recipes for cordials vary widely. I'll share the basics with you on the facing page, and then you can take off on your own.

> ### CHERRY CORDIAL
> *Good Housekeeping*, June 1888

Technically a bounce, recipes for cordials & bounces haven't changed since this recipe was recorded.

"To six pounds of cherries add three pounds of sugar and one gallon of whiskey. Shake the jar often for the first three weeks, then bottle. It will be fit for use in a month, and the longer it is kept the better it is."

CORDIALS & BOUNCES

FRESH FRUIT CORDIAL

There are two schools of thought on how to make cordials. I'll give you both; either method is fine. Feel free to experiment with the recipe by combining different fruits and adding sugar to your taste, but do not alter the ratio of fruit to vodka. Summer cordials will be ready to drink come winter, but they will sing for you if you can wait at least nine months.

2 cups fresh fruit, pitted, peeled and sliced as needed
1 cup sugar (I use less, but most folks prefer this amount)
2 cups 100 proof vodka

First method: Soak the fruit in the sugar a couple hours until the fruit releases its liquid and then add the mixture to the vodka. Mix well, and pour into a clean glass jar. Keep it in a dark cabinet and shake daily for the first couple weeks, if you can remember. Decant the liquid after about 2 months. Discard the fruit? Are you nuts? If it's not mushy, store in the fridge and make pies with it, eat on ice cream, etc. Store the racked cordial in a clean glass jar away from light.

Second method: Soak the fruit in the vodka as above and then make a sugar syrup with 1 cup sugar dissolved in ½ cup water. Add the cooled syrup to the cordial after the fruit is strained.

Author's note: Don't peel plums, but do peel peaches, apricots and nectarines. Raw elderberries are slightly toxic, they must be made into a cooked syrup before using in a cordial.

When the Children Begin to Ask for Coffee—

GIVE THEM
DRINKET
The Children's Beverage
MADE IN THE CUP

FRESH FRUIT BOUNCE

Same as a cordial only it's made with all or part brandy or whiskey. Cherry bounce is delicious as is blackberry. You can also layer a bounce with a cordial. Peach-raspberry is especially stunning. Make a sliced peach bounce with brandy. Peach tends to oxidize and turn brown at room temperature, so age and store this one refrigerated. When ready to serve, pour a little of the peach bounce into your cordial glass, then slowly add some red raspberry cordial. The raspberry will sit on top of the peach and the flavor combination is divine.

MONTH OF
J U N E

No, you cannot live on kisses,
Though the honeymoon is sweet,
Harken, brides, a true word this is,
Even lovers have to eat.

nd what do they eat, these lovers? Well. Besides strawberries and champagne ... they eat all manner of greens, scallions, peas plucked from the trellis, baby beets, salads of all sorts, radishes, cucumbers, squash, wax beans, robbed potatoes, lots of garlic, cherries, blueberries, rhubarb. You know what else lovers eat? Pie! In fact, if you're in search of love, there's no better way to find your perfect match than with the offering of a flaky-crusted cherry pie. June is a busy month; let's get to work.

A Flapjack

TAKE almost any self-assured lover, brown him over the fire of uncertainty first on one side of his nature, then give him a sudden turn and brown him on the other.

If you are pleased with the result and desire to incorporate him into your life, remove him to a place of safety before his interest has a chance to scorch; butter him with kindness and sweeten him well.

MONTH OF
J U N E

GARLIC SCAPE PESTO

Blink your eyes and the best food in the garden has come and gone.
Garlic scapes are the flower stalks of hardneck variet-
ies of garlic, and they're ready when they're ready and
you should be too. June to early July is when you'll see
them in the markets, depending on where you live. They
start out curled, then straighten and ultimately grow
little seed bulbs on the ends. Pick them while they're
tender, when they're curled like a pig's tail, and use in
place of garlic. If you see scapes in the market, grab
them. They'll keep in the vegetable bin of your fridge
for weeks, but to insure a good supply all winter, freeze
pesto in 4 ounce jars. The parsley is optional, but it
makes for a lovely spread that's not too terribly strong.

10 garlic scapes, cut into one-inch pieces
Handful Italian parsley (optional)
½ cup grated good Parmesan or Asiago cheese
Handful lightly roasted walnuts
Olive oil, extra virgin

Whirl the garlic scapes, parsley and walnuts in the food processor until smooth.
Add cheese and slowly drizzle in enough olive oil to make a nice spreadable
paste to eat on bruschetta, pasta, or veggies.

GARLIC SCAPE PESTO-STUFFED
CHICKEN BREASTS

Melt a little butter in a cast iron skillet and set your oven to
350º. Butterfly one chicken breast per person or just cut a pocket
into the middle of each. Stuff with a tablespoon of garlic scape
pesto and close up well. Dip breast in butter then roll in bread
crumbs that have been seasoned with a little salt and pepper.
Return to the skillet and bake until browned and crispy,
with an internal temperature of 165º. It'll take about 30-45
minutes depending on size and number in pan.

MONTH OF
J U N E

A peace-offering to balance out the feminine leanings of this book, I come bearing he-man gifts. Salads, actually. Guy salads, if you can fathom it. This annoying, yet entertaining cookbook has some excellent recipes contributed by famous man-cooks ranging from Houdini to a French ambassador.

FRENCH RADISH SALAD

"The French ambassador presents his compliments and begs to state that he does not believe that any dish, or food, is more palatable than a salad of radishes, the radishes to be cut in very thin slices and to be seasoned with the usual salad dressing." (See below.)

FRENCH DRESSING

"This salad (above) will be at its best if the foundation, upon which the thin slices of radish are placed, is made of small crisp leaves of romaine. The usual dressing — French, of course — is prepared in this way: To one tablespoonful of lemon or vinegar add three table-spoonsful of the best olive oil, a dash of black pepper, and a half teaspoonful of salt. Beat well with a silver fork, and add enough paprika to give it a ruddy color, and a rich flavor. If the salad dish is rubbed with garlic it will do no great harm to the mixture!" (1922)

MONTH OF
J U N E

WILTED LETTUCE (A LA RED CREEK)

Terry Ramsey, known now for penning the 1926 book entitled "The History of the Motion Picture," contributes this yummy southern salad.

"In behalf of my favorite fodder, the tender leafling lettuce that's newly sprung in June, I am pleased to present a method of introducing it to the human system with a maximum effectiveness. It is said that this dish comes to us from the Hessians. If this be treason let us make the most of it.

Having obtained the lettuce, young and tender and fresh from the patch, plucked before it is yet headstrong, toss it into a bucket of cold water to crisp it. Repairing to the kitchen, place on the hot stove a skillet and heave into it a good sized cupful of chopped bacon. Let it fry thoroughly. Add a dessert spoonful of salt, a pinch of mustard, a couple of tablespoonsful of granulated sugar and good cider vinegar in quantity slightly in excess of the bacon fat. Let it simmer smartly until well blended. Meanwhile lay out the lettuce in noble heaps on the plates on which it is to be served. Chop up a handful of green onions, a bit of the tops will do no harm, and at the last moment stir them into the concoction in the skillet. While the whole is sizzling and boiling vigorously, pour the mixture over the lettuce, using a spoon to apportion the nifty bits of bacon about, and serve forthwith. By this method one can take aboard amazing quantities of lettuce, which is most desirable in view of the fact that this gentle herb contributes strongly to the summer languor when taken in adequate quantities." (1922)

Author's note: We call this a "killed" salad where I come from, in the southern Appalachian mountains. Your arteries will thank you for being conservative with the bacon grease. A pinch of salt is plenty.

MONTH OF J U N E

ANNA'S CREAM OF PEA SOUP
Chester County Recipes, 19teens

"Shell half a peck of green peas, wash the pods, wash the pods, put them into the soup kettle with plenty of water, boil until tender; drain and throw away pods. Put the peas into this water and boil them three-quarters of a hour. Take out one cup of the peas and mash the rest through a sieve into the soup kettle. Add three pints rich milk and the cup of peas, then let it come to a boil. Rub together 2 tablespoonsfuls of

The Pea. The Pewee.

butter and 2 of flour to a smooth paste and stir into the soup. Add a tablespoonful of chopped parsley, season with salt and pepper. A tablespoon of white sugar and a sprig of mint are pleasant additions."

Author's note: Rich milk is whole milk (top cream is shaken into milk). If you don't have fresh peas, frozen will do. Simmering the pea pods adds lots of flavor. Do try it.

CREAM OF PEA VARIATION

Shell enough organic peas to render you two cups. Simmer the shells 30 minutes in enough water to cover, then strain. Cook the peas in the strained broth about 5 minutes. Add a cup of whole milk, salt and pepper to taste, and a leek or several scallions sautéed in a bit of butter. Remove a couple spoonfuls of the peas, then purée the remainder of the soup. Garnish with remaining peas and either fresh tarragon or chopped mint leaves. Pea shoots make a fine topping as well.

MONTH OF JUNE

ROASTED & SMASHED ROBBED POTATOES

Sometimes, the best thing you can do with a really great potato is to get out of its way and just give it a roast. If you planted your potatoes in March, you'll have baby potatoes mid-June. You can carefully rob a couple from each plant without doing any harm. If you don't grow your own, find some early potatoes from your local farmers. They're now available in every hue and size. (See resources, page 146 for a good place to order seed potatoes.)

HARTER'S A NO. 1 FLOUR
Makes Snow-white Bread.

Preheat oven to 400º. Toss whole fingerling or similarly sized cubed potatoes with a drizzle of extra virgin olive oil. Sprinkle with coarse salt and some fresh ground pepper and place on a baking sheet lined with parchment. Bake at 400º until potatoes are golden-brown.

To make pan-fried smashed potatoes, boil young fingerling potatoes until just tender. Place in a frying pan with a little melted butter. Smash potato with a glass just until skin breaks and pan-fry on either side until brown, then sprinkle with coarse salt.

Shoemaker turned mayor of Detroit and then governor of Michigan, Hazen Pingree, is a folk hero whose message we ought to be listening to right about now, more than a century hence. Detroit was hit hard in the panic of 1893 when stocks plummeted, banks closed, and millions of Americans lost their jobs and consequently starved to death. Not one to let his Detroit residents suffer so, Mayor Pingree called upon owners of idle vacant urban lots to donate the use of their land in order to create community gardens.

"Potato-patch" Pingree gave thousands of unemployed workers the chance to grow tons of produce in hundreds of urban gardens over the next few years, staving off hunger, and giving the down-and-out a meaningful opportunity to help themselves.

ALL BUTTER FLAKY PIE CRUST

You're going to need a good pie crust recipe, and this one is flaky, tender, and tasty. Pie is all the rage these days; I know this because every summer my family hosts a retro pie contest in Asheville. Last August, 120 participants judged about 80 homemade pies. Competition is fierce for vintage prizes in about 20 categories, and each year the pies get better and more creative. A great crust will win you a pie contest! This recipe makes a couple 9 or 10-inch shallow pie pan crusts with enough left over for decorative pastry cutouts.

3 cups all purpose flour	1 cup unsalted butter
¾ tsp. salt	½ cup ice water
Pinch baking powder	Fresh lemon juice

Mix the dry ingredients. Chop your butter into little cubes and cut half of it into the flour with a pastry cutter or the tips of your fingers until the mixture resembles coarse crumbs. Add the rest of the butter and mix it in until it's the size of small peas. Work fast; the fat must stay cold. Squeeze lemon juice into ice water and drizzle onto your flour mixture while tossing with a fork. Add only enough water so that your dough just sticks together when squeezed. Now toss your dough onto the counter and quickly smear just a couple times with the heel of your hand. Form dough into 2 patties, cover with plastic wrap, and refrigerate an hour or, better yet, overnight. Let the chilled dough sit a few minutes, then roll from the center out, giving it a quarter turn every couple rolls. You want it to be about 1½ inches bigger than the top of your pie plate. Trim jagged edges and place crust in pie pan. Fill your pie, flute the crust, and let it chill about 30 minutes before baking.

Pie Queens, 2008 contest

To make pastry cutouts, roll your dough and cut with leaf or other decorative cutters. Brush a bit of water on the back of your cutout and then press lightly onto your crust before baking.

MONTH OF
J U N E

Ring Ring.

"Hello?"

"I HIT THE MOTHERLODE ... YOU GOTTA MEET ME RIGHT NOW! BRING ALL THE BUCKETS AND BASKETS YOU CAN FIND. WE HAVE PIE-FIXINS!"

"The motherlode of what, Brookes?"

"Cherries, millions and millions of ripe cherries, sour *and* sweet!"

And so it went on a Wednesday morning in early June last summer. Turns out Brookes had been scoping out the trees in the front yard of her neighbor's house for years, just waiting for an opportunity to pilfer the orphaned ripe cherries (with permission, of course). If you don't pick cherries just as soon as they ripen, the birds will; so we acted fast and gathered gallons and gallons of the little red dar-

lings, thus marking the beginning of our summer of fruit pilfering. A pie made from found fruit beats out all other pies, in my estimation. So I'm sharing with you the recipe for Double Sour Cherry Amaretto Pie from my *Lost Art of Pie* book that has garnered several blue ribbons at county fairs.

DOUBLE SOUR CHERRY AMARETTO PIE

4 cups pitted sour cherries plus their juices
¾ cup sugar (adjust according to cherries)
2½ Tbs. cornstarch
½ cup dried sour cherries
3 Tbs. Amaretto almond liqueur

Soak dried cherries in warm Amaretto 2 hours. Toss pitted fresh cherries with sugar and cornstarch; then add dried cherries. Pour mixture into a 9-inch unbaked crust, and weave top with lattice strips. Bake in bottom third of a 400º oven about 45 minutes until filling bubbles in the center of the pie. If crust is browning too quickly, cover loosely with a piece of foil. Don't let anybody pilfer this pie as it cools on your windowsill!

MONTH OF
J U N E

Hilarious Refreshment Champagne Ice
I Go A-Marketing, 1900

"A champagne ice isn't such a high-roller refreshment as it sounds. To begin with, it's a rank solecism to freeze any but the most inexpensive of champagnes, and then you don't require many other good things for your ice — the champagne is enough in itself. You just make a very strong and sweet lemonade — a quart of it and half freeze it; then pour in the champagne and wholly freeze the mixture. Get the champagne into the freezer as soon as you can after it is opened before its volatile gas escapes. If you prefer a more hilarious refreshment just keep on with your use of intoxicants by adding after the champagne a wineglassful of brandy.

While we are on the subject of frozen champagne let me speak a good word for champagne with strawberries. Freeze together a quart of champagne and a pint of sugar syrup. Just at the last add one pint of strawberries which have been halved and quartered and marinated in a little brandy and sugar for about fifteen minutes. Strawberries used in this way will make you ready to declare that till you tried it you didn't know how to live." (1900)

Ouch! Physics and Beauty
Good Housekeeping, 1894

Study yourself in the glass and decide what is the greatest defect in your figure. It may be that you are short waisted, with too much flesh in that region; if so, do not attempt to correct the defect by lacing. The figure will not bear depression at one point without a corresponding increase in size at another. Thousands of ladies are wearing harmful devices so that they may appear to have well-developed figures, but these are only a mockery and a snare. They do not deceive the eye according to the intention, and if long persevered in, they produce atrophy of the breasts, which makes their proper development a well-nigh hopeless case.

MONTH OF
J U N E

CHERRY STRUDEL
Aunt Babette's Cook Book, 1889

"Make a dough of one pint of flour, a pinch of salt and a little lukewarm water; do not make it too stiff, but smooth. Slap the dough on the table back and forth. To do this take the dough in your right hand and hit the table with a vengeance as hard as you can. Do this repeatedly for about fifteen minutes. Now put the dough in a warm, covered bowl and set it in a warm place and let it rest for half an hour. In the meantime stem and pit two quarts of sour cherries. Grate into them some stale bread (about a plateful); also the peel of half a lemon, and mix. Add half a pound or more of sugar, some ground cinnamon and about four ounces of pounded sweet almonds, and mix all thoroughly. Now cover your kitchen table with a clean tablecloth, one that is large enough to cover it entirely, and sift flour over the whole of it. Roll out the dough as thin as possible, lay aside the rolling pin and pull, or rather stretch the dough as thin as tissue paper. In doing this you will have to walk all around the table, for when well stretched it will cover more than the size of an ordinary table.

Pull off all of the thick edge, for it must be very thin to be good. Pour a little melted goose oil or butter over this, and sprinkle the bread crumbs, sugar, almonds, cherries, etc., over it. Roll the strudel together into a long roll. To do this properly, take hold of the cloth with both hands and roll up carefully; have ready a long baking pan well greased with either butter or goose fat; fold the strudel into the shape of a pretzel, pull the cloth to the edge of the table, dump the strudel into the pan as quickly as possible, securing the edges well so as not to have the juice escape, butter the top also and bake to a light brown; baste often while baking. Eat warm."

Author's note: Fun reading, but try at your own risk!

Have a Strudel-Stretching Party

53

MONTH OF
J U L Y

arly in July the good housekeeper begins to think of her jelly and jam. At least that's what the 1888 *Good Housekeeping* proclaims. I must be an extra good housekeeper because I think of jelly and jam with the first strawberries of May. At any rate, July is a fantastic fruit month. Peaches, plums, blueberries, blackberries are begging to be bought, gathered or pilfered and made into pies, ice cream, cordials and JAM!

Summer vegetables are bursting forth as well. There are squash, beans, cukes, onions, carrots, tomatoes, potatoes, peppers, pesto (OK, not a vegetable), and herbs clamoring for your culinary attention.

Brandy Cherries, 1853—"Take the nicest carnation cherries, and trim them, leaving a short stem to keep in the juice; wash and wipe them tenderly, and put them into wide-mouthed bottles. Make a good syrup, and, when it is nearly done, add a pint and a half of French brandy to one pint of syrup; mix it thoroughly, and, when cold, pour it over the cherries. If carefully sealed, the fruit will be good for years."

Don't Drink Black Wine!

To detect Sugar of Lead in Wines.—The tincture of orpiment converts wine so adulterated to a black color.   ~*The New Household Receipt-Book*, 1853

Very toxic, sugar of lead (lead acetate) has a sweet taste and was unfortunately used by unscrupulous wine purveyors to flavor wine during the time of this writing. But assuming that folks would have had orpiment, an even more toxic chemical, lying about the house is downright interesting. Orpiment is an arsenic sulfide that was used up until the 19th century by many a sickened artist as a yellow paint pigment.

MONTH OF
J U L Y

You'd think vintage agricultural journals like *Woman's Farm Journal* and *The Farmer's Wife* would be bursting with kitchen garden recipes in the summer months. Well, they're not. And do you know why? If you pick or purchase sun-ripened, old-timey varieties of produce adapted to your particular region, you don't need to do anything to get them to taste good. Sweet corn tastes best as is. Put the water on to boil, then pick what you need for dinner, cook a few minutes, and you won't even care about butter or salt. Most vintage cookbooks contain few vegetable or meat recipes, because, back then, mom knew how to prepare them simply. But when it came to pickling or baking, a little instruction was helpful then, as now. You won't find many produce recipes in these pages for the same reason, but you might enjoy a few condiments made from garden goodies.

LIME BASIL PESTO

1½ cups lime basil leaves
½ cup flat leaf parsley
½ cup grated Parmesan
Squirt of fresh lime juice
¼ cup pine nuts or walnuts, toasted
2 cloves garlic
¼-½ cup extra virgin olive oil

Combine all ingredients except oil in food processor and chop. With machine running, drizzle in enough oil to achieve the texture you like. This pesto loves yellow squash, crusty bread, or pasta.

BLACKBERRY BALSAMIC GRILLING GLAZE

¾ cup seedless blackberry pulp
1 Tbs. balsamic vinegar
3 Tbs. honey
Salt and pepper to taste

What could be simpler? Combine ingredients in saucepan and heat a couple minutes. You can add a little olive oil if you like. Brush on chicken as you grill. Interesting on salmon as well.

MONTH OF JULY

NASTURTIUM VINEGAR
Mrs. Allen's Cook Book, 1917

"Loosely fill a pint jar with fresh nasturtium leaves. Cover with cider vinegar, put on top, let stand in a sunny place for three weeks, and strain. A few peppercorns can be added if desired. Other herb vinegars that can be made the same way: Tarragon, mint, chervil."

CATHY'S NASTURTIUM BUTTER

My friend, Cathy, serves this vibrant old-time savory butter in her Asheville bakery along with her lunch fare. I like it on fresh corn or as a spread on a cucumber sandwich. Here's the recipe in Cathy's words:

"It is really simple... I just mince nasturtium flowers and mix that in with softened butter. Proportions might be 20 or more flowers to one cup of salted butter. It is especially good on spinach feta bread. I have also served it on burger buns for veggie burgers, and I have swirled it into carrot soup right before serving. It's extra nice if you have a whole flower that you can put on the side of the bowl of soup!" (See page 128 for a winter version of Cathy's carrot soup.)

PICKLED NASTURTIUM SEED
Good Housekeeping, July 1901

"In various gravies and sauces, nasturtium seeds prove an excellent substitute for capers. Gather the green seeds after the flowers dry off and before they grow large and ripe. Make a strong brine of salt and water and pour over the green seeds. Let them lie in this for two days, then put in cold water for twenty-four hours. Drain and pack in bottles, pour over them a scalding vinegar spiced with mace, peppercorns and cloves and slightly sweetened with white sugar. Allow the seeds to pickle a month before using them." (1901)

MONTH OF JULY

MOCK PORK
The Pure Food Cook Book, 1914

If you ever see a "mock" recipe in a vintage cook-book, perk up. Not to be outwitted by seasonal scarcities of food products, yesterday's accomplished cook could make anything taste like its authentic twin. Since late fall was hog-butchering time on the farm, fresh as well as preserved pork would have been long gone come summer, in the days before refrigeration. This particular recipe would be overcooked using today's summer squash varieties, so I'm including an updated recipe.

"Mock pork requires squash, but the white, summer variety. Select a nicely shaped, large squash. Be sure not to get one that looks at all yellow, for if you do it will have to be peeled, which is undesirable, as peeled squash is apt to fall to pieces in the cooking. Cut a circle with a sharp knife all around the squash, and remove, to enable you to scoop out the seeds; then fill with the following:

One pint of stale bread crumbs; one onion chopped fine ; one-half teaspoonful of powdered sage; a teaspoonful of dried mustard; two ounces of butter cut into small pieces; half a teaspoonful of salt and pepper. Mix thoroughly; moisten with two beaten eggs. After the squash is filled, replace the piece that was cut out, put into a baking pan, and cook for two hours. Use bacon or pork drippings to baste with. To make the gravy which should accompany it, fry a sliced onion golden brown in butter; add pepper and salt to taste, and half a pint of milk; stir constantly, cook until golden brown, and the consistency of thick cream. Put the baked squash on a hot platter; pile up a wall of apple sauce around it; mashed turnips and new potatoes are the nicest vegetables to serve with it." (1914)

STUFFED SUMMER SQUASH

Plunge little round zucchini and/or green patty pan squash into salted boiling water for one minute. Hollow out and fill with buttered bread crumbs, sautéed squash guts, onion, and garlic, anything else you can think of like bits of tomato or ham and a sprinkling of fresh thyme. Top with good grated Parmesan and place in a buttered baking pan. Bake at 375º until the squash browns nicely.

MONTH OF
J U L Y

NORTH WOODS SUCCOTASH
Good Housekeeping, April, 1890

Take a sturdy iron pot, slice some fat salt pork to line it;
Pour a little water in, just for gravy to refine it.
Turn your sweet corn in and cook. Just an hour and season lightly;
Butter, salt and pepper add, just to make the flavor sprightly.
Boil some tender garden beans, through and through, be sure you do it.
By this time the corn is fine; stir the well-cooked beans into it.
Put more salt and pepper in, butter just to give a flavor;
Cover up with pork and cook, one-half hour to give the savor.
Turn out hot and full of juice, and no doubt 'twill see your wishes.
This is what we eat in camp, one of Adirondack's dishes.

HOEING HIS ROW.

Hoeing his roe, the farmer boy
Whistles and sings in careless joy,
Nature smiling on every side,
Quickly the hours and moments glide;
Little of sorrow his spirits know
As gaily he labors and hoes his row.

Hoeing his row, in later years,
A buoyant hope his spirit cheers;
While blade and stalk grow green and strong,
He sings full many a lover's song;
And future pleasures brighter grow
As hoping he labors and hoes his row.

Hoeing his row in middle life
Away from the cares and angry strife,
A loving wife and children fair
His many joys and pleasures share;
Crops of plenty their wealth bestow,
As happy he labors and hoes his row.

Hoeing his row—the setting sun
Tells us his work will soon be done—
Peace and comfort crown his days,
And all who know him speak his praise;
Who would not change the world's vain show
For his simple joys, as he hoes his row?

Hoeing his row? His life is past,
His sweetest moments were his last;
He never sought for praise or fame,
But children's children bless his name;
Over his grave sweet breezes blow,
The faithful farmer has hoed his row.

Kansas City Journal, 1888

MONTH OF
J U L Y

"How would you like to be invited to eat dinner with this family? You would have baked ham, home-canned green beans, potatoes boiled in their jackets, mixed vegetables, salad, milk, biscuits with butter, and

Good food and plenty of it

custard. A well-balanced meal supplied from the farm. Farmers' families everywhere can have meals as appetizing as this one every day."

~Library of Congress, 1942

STUFFED PAN-FRIED SQUASH BLOSSOMS

Do your ungrateful neighbors bolt their doors when they see you coming toward them during squash season? Not only will you re-gain your popularity, you'll barely have enough zucchini for pickles when you discover these crunchy hot squash blossoms that are even better than squash. Serve them hot from the frying pan.

Pick either male or female squash blossoms in the late morning when fully opened, keeping an inch or two of stem attached. Check for bees, pick out the stamen, and gently rinse. Stuff with a spoonful of chevre (fresh goat cheese), or other cheese to your liking and a sprinkling of chopped fresh herbs. Fold the sides of the blossom around the filling. Dip in buttermilk and dredge in cornmeal seasoned with salt and pepper. Pan-fry in a bit of butter.

MONTH OF
J U L Y

REFRIGERATOR PICKLES

When cucumbers are in, they're invited to every meal at our house. I slice and marinate them about an hour with thinly sliced onion in a mixture of sherry vinegar, a drizzle of honey and a sprinkling of salt. If you can get a-hold of lots of cukes, then this recipe will keep in your fridge about a month. Feel free to adjust the sugar to your liking. Use fresh small pickling cucumbers, prickly Japanese cukes, or other varieties with small seeds.

2 lb. sliced FRESH cucumbers	¾ tsp. salt
1 large onion, thinly sliced	¾ cup sugar (or less)
1½ cups vinegar	¼ tsp. turmeric
½ tsp. each celery seed & mustard seeds	
Red pepper pod or ½ tsp. red pepper flakes	

Place cucumbers and onions in a ½ gallon canning jar. Heat remaining ingredients until sugar dissolves. Pour over vegetables. When cool, place lid on and refrigerate. They're best after a few days.

In some parts of Europe, it is customary for gardeners who rent land to consider the top soil as their personal property and to take this upper layer with them when they move.   Hagers-town Almanack, 1929

Suggestive Constitution for a Mother-Daughter Home Canning Club, 1915

"The purpose of this organization shall be to teach and encourage the home canning of those food products which are generally plentiful in summer but scarce in winter, and to bring about a closer friendship and cooperative spirit in rural and village communities."   ~*USDA* publication

Library of Congress, 1940

MONTH OF
J U L Y

Pickles come only partly by nature—they are born of work and worry.

CUCUMBER PICKLES
Good Housekeeping, July, 1901

"Always pick cucumbers in the early morning or late at night; gathering them under a hot sun often proves a death blow to the vines.

A day's picking of fine cucumbers, 250 dozen.

Choose the smallest cucumbers and absolutely perfect ones. Put a layer of cucumbers in a glass can and scatter through them fine strips of horseradish root. Mix a gallon of vinegar with half a gallon of water, add to it one cup of salt and pour it cold over the packed cucumbers. Fill the jar overflowing and seal immediately." (1901)

A PRICKLED PICKLE OF A WOMAN
Southern Field and Fireside, July 6, 1861

"... His wife was quite a different character. She was a good woman—in her way; had received her share of life's blessings, and with a devoted husband and a loving daughter to smooth the evening of her days, she ought to have been happy. But she was not. She belonged to the class of pickles, not preserves, and gave the impression as you looked upon her, that she had become thoroughly saturated with vinegar, or to change the figure, she was

> Like a hedgehog rolled up the wrong way,
> Tormenting himself with his prickles.

and thus delighting in her own unhappiness, she was never satisfied that any one should enjoy himself."

MONTH OF
J U L Y

WINDFALL PLUM SORBET

The pilfered fruit award goes to my friend, David. Last summer, he generously offered up the best plums I ever tasted from his backyard tree bursting with about a bazillion of the dark red fruits. They found their way into plum cake, cordial and plum brandy, pies, jams, and this gorgeous voluptuous, bright red sorbet.

2½ cups plum pulp from about 2 lb. fruit
Mint-infused simple syrup to taste
1 Tbs. Grand Marnier or plum cordial
A good squirt of fresh lemon juice

Make simple syrup by combining ½ cup sugar and ¼ cup water. Simmer until sugar is dissolved. Add a few fresh mint leaves, then let mixture cool. Purée pitted and sliced plums in a food processor or blender and strain through a sieve to remove skin if you like. (I prefer to leave the skins in.) Combine plum purée, Grand Marnier, and lemon juice. Remove mint and pour in syrup to taste. Chill completely and then freeze in your ice cream machine. The liqueur is optional, but a little alcohol gives the sorbet a creamy texture.

H AND in hand with summer comes
The happy family called the Plums,
Some dressed in purple, some in red;
They're very pretty and well bred.

~*Mother Earth's Children*, 1914

KIRSCH SHERBET
I Go A-Marketing, 1900

"A Kirsch sherbet is a delicacy that doesn't put itself in the way of ordinary mortals every day in the week. That's why its welcome is a soulful one when it does appear. You have a pint of Chablis and a pint of any preferred fruit syrup, which you freeze. Then at the last there is added to it half a pint of Kirschen-wasser." (1900)

Author's note: Make a fruit sorbet as above, and for every cup of sweetened purée, add a cup of Chablis and 2 Tbs. Kirsch. Taste before sending it to the ice cream freezer.

Hauling peaches to the cannery.

ROASTED PEACHES

If you don't have a peach tree, buy a big basket of wonderful freestone peaches at your local farmer's market. When they're just ripe, slice them in half and roast skin-side up on a parchment-lined sheet pan in a 350º oven for about an hour. Slip skins off and freeze individually on the sheet pan. Bag the peaches and then, in the dead of winter, pull them out. Whirl them in your food processor just as they are for a low calorie, healthful frozen sorbet. Top with a drizzle of your peach raspberry cordial.

SUMMER LEMON CORNMEAL PLUM CAKE

Simple, quick, plummy and just fabulous. The kind of cake you can feel good about eating every day during plum season.

1 cup all purpose flour	½ cup whole milk
½ cup freshly ground cornmeal	4 Tbs. unsalted butter, melted
2 tsp. baking powder	3 Tbs. butter, softened
½ tsp. salt	1 large egg
½ cup white sugar	Zest of an organic lemon
¼ cup brown sugar, packed	Plums, 8 large or about 12 small

Preheat oven to 400º. Butter two pie plates or an oblong baking dish. Combine milk, melted butter, egg and zest. Whisk until blended. In a separate bowl, combine flour, baking powder, salt and white sugar. Add wet ingredients to dry and stir until blended. Spread batter into prepared pans, and place halved and pitted plums with cut sides up around top of batter. Mix together the 3 Tbs. softened butter and brown sugar and smear that mixture on top of each plum. Bake until lightly browned, about 30 minutes.

MONTH OF AUGUST

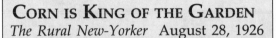

"From now until frost King Corn should have a prominent place in our daily menus. We will serve corn for breakfast. How? In corn fritters, in griddle cakes and waffles, with omelets and scrambled eggs and fried with bacon. You won't need a recipe for corn fritters and griddle cakes. Just add a cup or more of left-over corn to your favorite fritter recipe." (1926)

We'll be serving corn for lunch; we'll be serving corn for dinner; we'll be serving corn for dessert. Guess what we'll be having for snacks? Corn! Corn! Corn! Corn salad, corn soup, corn puffs, escalloped corn, corn bread, corn pudding, cornmeal cookies, popcorn balls, and just plain old corn on the cob.

And tomatoes. Oh, mercy me, there's nothing like a sun-warmed meaty pink heirloom Brandywine tomato coaxed from the vine and onto the plate. August is surely a time for passionate eating.

To Keep Crows from Corn 1853

—Take a quart of train oil, and as much turpentine and bruised gunpowder; boil them together, and, when hot, dip pieces of rags in the mixture, and fix them on sticks in the field. About four are sufficient for an acre of corn.

~*The Household Receipt-Book*

Author's warning: Need I say, *DON'T!!!!*

MONTH OF AUGUST

The following recipes are from *The Rural New-Yorker*, August, 1926

GREEN CORN SOUP

Boiled corn cobs make the best soup stock. Freeze in pint jars for flavorful winter soups and stews. Rich milk includes top cream; use whole milk. Green corn refers to young field corn, common before sweet varieties became popular, so you can omit the sugar from these recipes.

"You will need one pint of green corn pulp, one pint of rich milk, one teaspoon salt, one eighth teaspoon white pepper, one teaspoon sugar, one teaspoon flour and one tablespoon butter. Cover the corn cobs with boiling water and boil 30 minutes; strain. To one pint of this corn liquor add the corn pulp and cook 15 minutes. Add the seasonings and the scalded milk. Thicken with melted butter and flour, thinned with a little milk; cook five minutes longer. Serve hot with crackers." (1926)

GREEN CORN PUFFS

"You will need two eggs, one cup milk, two cups grated corn, ¼ teaspoon paprika, ½ teaspoon salt, a few grains of cayenne and some grated cheese. Beat the eggs until light; add the milk, corn, salt, pepper and cayenne. Grease well six custard cups. Fill them part full of the mixture and place in a pan of hot water. Add one tablespoon grated cheese to each cup. Bake in a moderate oven until firm. Turn out on a hot platter and serve with tomato." (1926)
Author's note: Sharp cheddar cheese, bake at 350º, a greased muffin tin is fine.

ESCALLOPED CORN

"You will need one teaspoon salt, one eighth teaspoon pepper, two tablespoons flour, one cup bread crumbs, one tablespoon butter, six ears of cooked corn, ½ cup milk, three tablespoons cream and one teaspoon sugar. Cut the corn from the cob. Mix corn with salt and pepper, flour and sugar; add the milk and cream. Melt the butter, mix with the bread crumbs and cover the bottom of a pudding dish with them; add the corn mixture and cover with the rest of the crumbs. Bake in a moderate oven 20 minutes. Serve hot." (1926)

MONTH OF
AUGUST

CORN IN CASSEROLE
Practical Recipes, 1909

"1 tomato and 1 medium-sized onion sliced and stewed in butter the size of an egg, until well cooked. Take 4 or 5 good-sized ears of corn, cut through the center of grains and scrape out. Add this with 1 green pepper chopped fine to the tomato with plenty of salt and pepper and a dash of cayenne. Cook in casserole a little while and add the last thing, a cup of cream. Make hot and dish up." (1909)

Author's note: You can omit the cream; tastes fine without it.

GREEN CORN FRITTERS
Chester County Recipes, 19teens

Also called mock oysters or oyster corncakes, this old standard is just as good made with zucchini. Beat the egg a bit, add to the corn and milk mixture, then add your flour. (19teens)

"Grate 4 ears of corn, season with salt and pepper, a very little milk and just enough flour to hold them together, with one egg. Fry one tablespoon at a time in butter like you do oysters." (19teens)

Courtesy Library of Congress

Young boys shucking corn, 1915.

MONTH OF AUGUST

MAUDIE'S HALF-RUNNER BEANS

Here's my favorite August meal in the whole world. My West Virginia grandmother, Maudie, used to whip up this summer feast in her airy, sun-filled 1920s kitchen.

Half-runner beans with tomato and onion, Silver Queen corn on the cob, new potatoes with butter (cooked on top of the beans), plate-sized slices of Beefsteak tomatoes, buttermilk biscuits, and a smoked pork chop.

Grandmother picked our meal from her garden, and my sisters and I would string the beans and shuck the corn; then we'd watch with rapt attention as she rolled out and carefully cut her delicious southern buttermilk biscuits. To make Maudie's beans, choose an old-time variety of meaty bean with large seeds and strings. You heard me right, strings. We're partial to Greasy Cut-Short cornfield pole beans here in the Southern Appalachian mountains. My grandmother grew an early variety of half-runners. Your area has its own traditional pole bean worth seeking out as well.

Okay, grab a cold drink and find a nice place to sit outside in the shade where you can hear summer's critters chattering. An old green metal glider or a porch swing will do just fine. Settle your big yellow pyrex bowl filled with string beans in your lap. After pulling the string off each side of the beans, snap them a few times (don't cut with a knife, you'll slice up the beans). Now go into the kitchen and fry up a couple slices of good lean bacon in a saucepan. Add your beans and cover with water. Simmer anywhere from 30 minutes to 2 hours, depending on where you're from. Let me just say that if you're from West Virginia, you will probably slow cook the beans about 45 minutes. Head south and you'll add on an hour. Don't let the water boil out. There should be about ½ cup of pot likker left in the pan when they're done.

Here's the important part. Chop up the best vine-ripened tomato you can get your hands on, along with a freshly dug onion if you have one. Serve the green beans topped with a great big spoonful of the tomato-onion mixture.

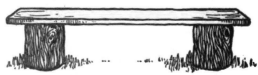

MONTH OF AUGUST

ROASTED TOMATOES

Here's what usually happens during a season of tomato harvesting and preserving at our house. First, eat them on everything you can think of, then cook them down for hours to make sauce out of them to can or freeze, then move on to plain unseasoned sauce, canned diced tomatoes, whole tomatoes, and finally to taking the cores out of a tomato and freezing the dern thing whole. To my good fortune, various types of tomato blights in our air and soil have encouraged me to grow backup varieties of plum and cherry tomatoes that flourish in any environment. And do they ever flourish. In desperation, I happened on this method of roasting them and now, the only tomatoes I can are the too-few heirlooms that survive our daily scarfing. Cherry tomatoes and plum tomatoes roast best, but any fresh tomato will do.

Cover a large parchment-lined baking sheet with stalks and leaves of fresh herbs, trimmed fresh from your garden (or someone else's). A mix of basil, thyme, oregano and rosemary is good. Cut your tomatoes in half and arrange them cut side up over the herbs. Throw on some chopped fresh garlic,

Courtesy Library of Congress

drizzle with a couple tablespoons of good extra virgin olive oil, then sprinkle very lightly with kosher (coarse) salt and some grindings of good pepper. The baking part will vary with your tomato variety, but I generally bake at 250º for about two hours until tomatoes are shrunken but not dry and lightly caramelized, the edges just a bit browned.

Let the roasted tomatoes cool on the baking sheet and then stick the whole pan in the freezer. Peel frozen tomatoes from the herbs and then store in quart jars or plastic bags in your freezer.

Use your roasted tomatoes on the top of pizza, tossed with pasta, in soups, paella, winter salads, any place you'd use a tomato.

MONTH OF AUGUST

BOYS & GIRLS IN THE GARDEN

From "Brief Bits"
Farm and Home, August, 1915

Emma Geiger, Iowa, has only her little sisters for pets. Emma is one of our gardeners. Last summer she raised beans and turnips, and she has a garden this year also.

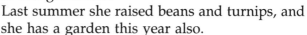

From "The Boys and Girls Page," *Rural New-Yorker*, August, 1926

July 29. Rained all night and day. Had one of the harses shod and picked berries. Cleaned my room and the hall this afternoon and hoed my garden this evening.
August 2. Very hot and sultry this forenoon, followed by a thunderstorm. Did a big washing while folks went to town. Mowed this afternoon. Podded peas for canning.
My diary signing off, Totsie , New York

LIMA BEANS
Us Two Cook Book, 1909

Another summer vegetable inspiration from my grandmother. She'd cook her giant Fordhook limas as in this recipe, only, after draining, she added a tiny pat of butter and let the beans scorch just a little before adding a splash of Guernsey cream. The flavor is exquisite, like roasted chestnuts.

"Put the lima beans into salted boiling water, and cook until tender, then drain off the water. Moisten them with butter, and season with salt and pepper; and add, if convenient, a little hot cream or cover with white sauce." (1909)

The Creoles have an old adage that "Nature itself tells us what to eat," in the various vegetables and fruits of each season, and in the varieties of fish and fresh meat that are particularly adapted to each clime.   ~*The Picayune Creole Cook Book, 1922*

MONTH OF AUGUST

To get along without hurrying, begin sooner.

"Devilled" Crab
Practical Recipes, 1909

"Boil crab and remove flesh from shell, chop fine. Brown a lump of butter the size of a large egg, add a teaspoon of flour and a pinch of celery salt, and a dash of red pepper. Let one small onion chopped fine and a bit of parsley simmer in the brown butter a few moments, then add the crab with a small glass of dry sherry, and a cup of cream. Fill the crab shell with this mixture and cover with cracker crumbs and a lump of butter. Brown in a quick oven. Delicious." (1909)

Household Hints

Four or five common playing marbles in the bottom of a kettle of boiling fruit juice by their constant motion will prevent scorching and make unnecessary constant stirring. ~*Practical Recipes*, 1909

Watermelon seed tea is an old remedy for dropsy. Two tablespoonfuls of the seed may be infused in a pint of hot water and left covered for an hour or two. Dose, a wineglassful or less three or four times daily. ~*Good Housekeeping*, August 1887

To keep cabbages throughout the winter:
• Cut off the stems, take off the outer leaves and then wrap each head in paper. They are then ready for packing in boxes of any size and should be put in a frostproof cellar.
• Cabbages hung up by the roots in the cellar will keep for two or three months. ~*Woman's Farm Journal*, December 1906

MONTH OF AUGUST

DOG-DAYS

Now flam'd the dog-star's unpropitious ray,
Smote every brain, and wither'd every bay;
Sick was the sun, the owl forsook his bower,
The moon-struck prophet felt the madding hour.

Alexander Pope.

BLACKBERRY TARTS WITH SOUR CREAM CRUST
Farm and Home, August, 1926

"Stir into one cup sour cream, one-third teaspoon saleratus and a pinch of salt, and add enough flour to make a very stiff dough. Roll very thin, cut into rounds as for cookies and bake quickly. Thicken

(by bringing to a boil) a well-sweetened cup blackberry sauce with one teaspoon cornstarch wet with two tablespoons water. When cold spread on crust round and press over top another round. This crust is healthful and also excellent for pies when one has sour cream to use." (1926)

Author's note: Saleratus is baking soda. Bake crusts at 400° until lightly browned.

Another freak vegetable is reported from Michigan, where the to-
mato and eggplant were crossed. In the result, the tomato was
predominant. ~*Woman's Farm Journal* December, 1906

MONTH OF AUGUST

Twenty little jelly-glasses,
Twenty pots of jam,
Making other wealth than this
Appear a stupid sham.

RASPBERRY JAM

Commercial pectin products will insure a good set for your fruit jams, but
you'll pay a price in flavor and texture for that bit of security. What fol-
lows is a traditional European method for making fruit confitures. A con-
tent of 80% sugar is customary, but you can get away with 75%. Any
lower and you won't get a good set. Though I'm not a big fan of sweets
myself, a little dab of summer fruit confiture on a piece of artisan cheese is
about as good as food gets. This process takes practice to perfect, better to
undercook than to overcook. You do not want to caramelize the fruit.

2 lb. fresh red raspberries
24 oz. sugar
Juice of 1 lemon

Bring the berries, sugar, and lemon
juice to a boil in a wide saucepan and
refrigerate overnight in a covered ceramic bowl. Next day, bring fruit back
to a boil and cook until temperature
reaches 220° (not over) on a candy thermometer, or until the jam is "set." To
check for set, drizzle a spoonful of syrup
onto a frozen plate. Swipe your finger through the jam, if it stays put on either
side of the "swipe," then it's set. Now pour into sterilized jars and water-bath
can for 15 minutes, adjusting for altitude. Read up on canning please! Information is available through your local county extension office. (See resources, page
146, for a recommended canning book.)

MONTH OF AUGUST

Courtesy Library of Congress

RASPBERRY PECAN THUMBPRINT COOKIES

Old-timey nut grinders with the glass container and screw-on grinding lid create the perfect size nuts for the coating. Vanilla wafers (see page 145) also make good thumbprint cookies.

¾ cup unsalted butter, softened
¾ cup brown sugar, packed
1 egg, separated
1 cup chopped pecans
1 tsp. vanilla
Raspberry jam

2 cups all purpose flour
½ tsp. salt

Makes Fine
Nut Butter

Preheat oven to 350°. Cream butter and sugar, then beat in egg yolk and vanilla. Sift flour and salt and add to creamed mixture. Shape into 1-inch balls and dip first into beaten egg white, then pecans. Poke your thumb into center of each cookie and fill with a bit of jam. Bake about 12 minutes until lightly browned.

FALL

The golden-rod is yellow, the corn is turning brown;
The trees in apple orchards, with fruit are bending down.
By all these lovely tokens, September days are here,
With summer's best of wealth, and autumn's best of cheer.
~Helen Hunt Jackson, 1908

ndeed, now's the time to harvest summer's best of wealth for the do-with-less months of December through March. It's a great time for gathering mushrooms and nuts, clearing out your garden and sharing the extra fruits from your orchard with your neighbors. You might consider a visit to your local farm and tailgate markets for bulk produce to can, pickle, dry, jam and freeze. When I walk about our autumn neighborhood, my neighbors implore me, "Please ... take some apples!" Well I can't say no, but who wants to end up like this poor woman from 1887:

> She was at our house the other day—whining, as usual: The fruit season's all over with and I didn't get to can half I wanted to, and I feel *so* put out about it. I'm so rushed all the time I never get to do half I want to. Some days I just sit down and cry.

MINUTE BEER (NON-ALCOHOLIC)
The Farmers and Emigrants Complete Guide, 1856

An antique soda pop. And better for you, I might add. Saleratus was an early form of baking soda. Use as little as possible to create a fizz.

"To be made in such quantities as wanted for immediate use. Take as much water as may be wanted, say two quarts; four large spoonsful of molasses, same quantity of good vinegar, and half a spoonful of fine ginger; mix these well together in the water; then to this mixture add half of a large spoonful of saleratus in powder, and stir and drink when in a state of effervescence. This will be found not only a delicious drink in warm weather but also a healthy beverage. Vary the proportions of the articles, to be more or less, as may be the quantity of beer wanted." (1856)

MONTH OF SEPTEMBER

If I were a tailor, I'd make it my pride
The best of all tailors to be;
If I were a tinker, no tinker beside;
Should mend a tin kettle like me.

QUINCE LIQUEUR POTATION
I Go A-Marketing, 1900

Whatever a potation is, I'll have one. It sounds like a party. Quinces are back from the past and trees are again available at your favorite nursery. A curious fruit, they're loaded with fragrance, flavor, and pectin. You'll find them to be a welcome addition to fall jams and jellies and all sorts of fall dishes. If you live near a quince tree, you can make an easier version of this cordial by adding 3 cups grated, de-fuzzed quinces to a quart jar with 2 cups brandy or vodka, and, if you like, half a vanilla bean and a little piece of cinnamon stick. Add a sugar syrup made from one cup sugar and one cup water, boiled and cooled. Let the potation sit a month, then strain.

"Another delicious potation that will be found of use at all sorts of occasions is quince liqueur. Grate a sufficient number of quinces to make a quart of juice after it is squeezed

"It tastes like the auld country, shure."

through a jelly bag. With this juice mix a pound of sugar, six ounces of bitter almonds, bruised, a dozen whole cloves and a gill of brandy. Mix these all well together and set away in a demijohn for ten days at least. Then strain it through the jelly bag till it is perfectly clear, and bottle for use. Besides drinking this as a liqueur, you will find that you can vary and improve a number of your recipes for punch by adding just a suspicion of it to them." (1900)

MONTH OF SEPTEMBER

OYSTER PIE
I Go A-Marketing, 1900

I don't think you'll be making this one unless you're an obstinate sort of fellow. Being that type myself, I just spent hours giving this recipe a spin, and believe me, it's not worth it. However, I am now, officially, no longer one of the pitifuls who can't make a good puff paste, thanks to the recipe on the facing page. And that's one reason why I'm including this oyster pie recipe. The other reason is that oysters were much more plentiful 100 years ago than they are now, all kinds of species and sizes, from canned to fresh. Oyster recipes were as common then as pound cake recipes are now; and besides, this makes for fun reading.

"It's a thousand pities that everybody doesn't know how to make good puff paste, for without that knowledge it is impossible to make a good oyster pie; but in case you are an adept at puff paste making, just try concocting one some fine day. Line a pie dish with the paste and fill it with uncooked rice; butter the paste that covers the edge of the dish and lay a cover of puff paste over the pie; press the edges together a bit and trim them neatly. Meanwhile prepare a quart of oysters by draining them from their liquour and chopping them fine.

Mix a teaspoonful of cornstarch in a very little cold milk, and pour over slowly half a pint of boiling milk or cream; when it is thick and smooth add to it an ounce of butter. Season the oysters with salt and pepper, and stir them into the mixture; simmer for five minutes. When the pie-crust is done remove it from the oven, take off the top crust, turn out all the rice and fill the dish with the oysters; put on the cover again, and set in the oven to get thoroughly hot." (1900)

Campfire pot pie in a cast iron Dutch oven.

MONTH OF SEPTEMBER

CAMPFIRE BAKING

September's a great time for some outdoor live-fire cooking. There's nothing like a campfire to bring folks together, and it doesn't have to be a big production, especially if you live in a place where you can have a firepit in your yard. Anything that can be baked in an oven, can be baked in a campfire or wood burning fireplace.

To bake a pie, cake, biscuits, cornbread, etc., you'll need a 9-inch glass pie plate and a 12-inch cast iron Dutch oven with feet and a recessed lid. (See resources, page 146.) Place three canning jar rings in the bottom of your iron pot and preheat by setting it on a little pile of embers away from the flames. Now shovel some live coals on top. After about 20 minutes, lift off the lid (a lid lifter is nice, but a fireplace poker will do), and carefully place your pie in the oven. Replace the lid, add a few more embers on top, and bake the usual amount of time. Check after about 20 minutes to adjust your heat. A little charring adds to the charm of your masterpiece.

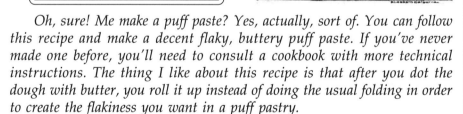

A FINE PUFF PASTE
Practical Recipes, 1909

Oh, sure! Me make a puff paste? Yes, actually, sort of. You can follow this recipe and make a decent flaky, buttery puff paste. If you've never made one before, you'll need to consult a cookbook with more technical instructions. The thing I like about this recipe is that after you dot the dough with butter, you roll it up instead of doing the usual folding in order to create the flakiness you want in a puff pastry.

"1 pound of sifted flour; 1 pound of butter; saltspoon of salt, and iced water. Divide the butter in 3 equal parts, rub one part thoroughly in the flour with salt, mix with the cold water a rather stiff dough, and roll out thin on a board; with a knife put little bits of butter over it. Roll it up and put in the ice chest for 20 minutes. Then repeat the process, rolling it again and let it remain on ice for 20 minutes more. Cut off enough for a pie and roll out lightly, handling it as little as possible." (Bake puff paste at 375º in top third of oven.)

MONTH OF SEPTEMBER

CREAM OF MUSHROOMS SOUP
What to Have for Luncheon, September, 1904

Cookbooks of this period assume you've been out mushroom hunting, but if perchance, you hunt your fungi at the local market, any mixture of mushrooms will do for this recipe. Note the method of thickening: "A tablespoon of butter rolled in one of flour." Rub the flour into the

butter and plop it into your soup or sauce. Voila! No lumps. Below is an updated version. You can substitute cream or half and half for part of the milk for a richer soup.

"Wash or wipe fresh mushrooms, cut fine, and sauté in two tablespoons of hot butter over a slow fire until the juice flows, adding cream gradually as the butter is absorbed; cook ten minutes, then add one quart of hot milk and simmer half an hour. Press through a sieve, heat again and thicken with a tablespoon of butter rolled in one of flour or cornstarch. Season with salt and pepper, and serve with croutons. The stems may be used for the soup and strained, and the peeled sautéed caps served in the tureen if preferred." (1904)

1 lb. mixed mushrooms	½ cup chicken broth
2 Tbs. butter	2 cups milk
2 shallots, chopped	¼ cup Marsala wine
Salt and pepper to taste	Nutmeg, freshly grated
1 Tbs. flour rubbed with 1 Tbs. butter	

Sauté shallots in butter, add thinly sliced or chopped mushrooms and cook 15 minutes. Pour in chicken broth and Marsala. When heated, stir in flour rolled in butter and stir well. Add as much milk as you like and season with salt and pepper. Grate just enough nutmeg into the soup to mystify your guests. Purée part of the mushrooms if you want a thicker soup.

MONTH OF SEPTEMBER

COTTAGER'S PIE
What to Have for Luncheon, 1904

"Cut fresh mushrooms in small pieces, sprinkle them with salt and pepper; sauté in butter. Cut thin slices of nice bacon in small pieces, put them in the bottom of a rather shallow baking-dish; on these put a layer of the mushrooms, and over these a layer of finely mashed and well-seasoned potatoes. Fill the dish in this way with a layer of mashed potatoes on top. Put bits of butter on top, cover, and bake half an hour in a moderately hot oven. When nearly done remove the cover and brown the top." (1904)

Note: Cook bacon before assembling.

Photo courtesy Renate Rikkers, former president of the Asheville mushroom club. The mushroom on the left looks to be the deadly "death cap."

Cautions 1916. "Unless you are absolutely sure that you know a mushroom when you see it, do not run the risk of gathering and using for food what you may think are mushrooms. A very large number of people are poisoned every year because of carelessness along this line. There are many other plants of the mushroom-toadstool varieties that are very poisonous, and they resemble the edible mushrooms very much."

~ *Agriculture, A Text for the School and Farm*, 1916

COOK ALL EDIBLE MUSHROOMS!

MONTH OF SEPTEMBER

CORNBREAD

You might as well call the southern Appalachian mountains Cornbread-ville; we are all about corn. The early pioneers grew plenty of it on newly logged mountain land and there were water-powered grist mills in every community with portable mills scat-tered here and about. Older farm women go on ... and on ... and on about how good the cornbread was "back then" from freshly milled local varieties of dent corn. They were right; fresh milled corn is nothing like store-bought. Buy your cornmeal from an historic mill if you can and keep it in the freezer. In the South, folks don't add sugar to their cornbread. The preferred method of baking is in a preheated cast iron skillet for a crunchy crust that begs to be slathered with butter and sorghum syrup or honey.

1½ cups stone-ground cornmeal	5 Tbs. unsalted butter
½ cup all purpose flour	1¼ cups buttermilk
2 tsp. baking powder	1 egg
¾ tsp. salt	Pinch soda

Melt butter in cast iron skillet in a preheated 450° oven. Mix dry ingredients in one bowl, and whisk together wet ingredients, including the melted butter, in another. Add wet to dry and stir just until blended. Pour back into hot buttered skillet and bake 25 minutes until nicely browned.

A men's cornhusking, 1940s

MONTH OF SEPTEMBER

BREAD MADE OF WOOD
The Farmers and Emigrants Complete Guide, 1856

"In times of great scarcity, and where famine threatens, it is well to know how to prepare a nutritious substance, which may go under the name of bread, from the beech and other woods destitute of turpentine. Take green wood, chop it into very small chips; or make it into shavings, which is better. Boil these three or four times, stirring them very hard during boiling. Dry them, and then reduce them to powder if possible; if not, as fine as you can. Bake this powder in the oven three or four times, and then grind it as you would corn. Wood thus prepared acquires the smell and taste of corn-flour. It will not ferment without the addition of leaven. The leaven prepared for corn-flour, is the best to use with it. It will form a spongy bread, and when much baked with a hard crust, is by no means unpalatable."

MAPLE ROASTED WINTER SQUASH

Easy, quick, healthy, and delicious. What more could you want? Any heirloom pumpkin or large meaty winter squash will do. My favorite for this recipe is a red kuri Japanese squash, also known as baby red hubbard.

Cut your pumpkin in half and scrape out the seeds and stringy pulp. Slice the flesh into "smiles" about an inch thick, leaving the skin on. In a large bowl, mix together:

¼ cup maple syrup	1 Tbs. balsamic vinegar
2 Tbs melted butter	Salt and pepper to taste
Pinch of cayenne or chili flakes	

Coat the squash with the butter mixture and place in a single layer onto a parchment or foil-lined baking sheet. Drizzle remaining liquid over the squash. Sprinkle with salt and pepper and bake at 375º on lower rack of oven until caramelized, 20 to 40 minutes.

MONTH OF SEPTEMBER

KITCHEN WISDOM

~There is nothing like settling with ourselves, as there 's a deal we must do without in this life.

~You cannot prevent the birds of sadness from flying over your head, but you may prevent them from stopping to build their nests there.

~The responsibility of tolerance lies with those who have the wider vision.

~George Eliot

~Some people are always grumbling because roses have thorns. I am thankful that thorns have roses.   ~Alphonse Karr

~To suspect a friend is worse than to be deceived by him. ~La Rochefoucauld

~To smile at the jest which plants a thorn in another's breast
is to become a principal in the mischief.   ~Sheridan

~Love and a cough cannot be hidden.

~Man's the head, but woman turns it.

~They love too much who die for love.

~You can't climb the Alps on roller skates.

MONTH OF SEPTEMBER

You either love fresh figs or you don't. If you love them and you have a little space, grow them if you can. Here in the North Carolina mountains, we get a late crop in September or October, right before the first fall freeze. Just as last year's crop of little green immature figs was about to be walloped by a frost, I learned a tidy little trick to hasten the ripening process from our local men's garden club. Put a dab of olive oil on the tip of each fig while still on the tree. In a few days, you'll have plump ripe figs.

ROASTED FIGS

Roasted figs are as good as food gets. They love pungent greens like watercress or arugula, goat cheese, toasted walnuts, pears and balsamic vinegar. Throw them in your salad, add to chicken or pork, or just eat them right out of the oven.

Preheat oven to 350º and cut fresh figs in half. Place cut side down on parchment and bake for 10 minutes or until they begin to release their juices. Flip over and cook about 30 minutes more until they are shrunken and caramelized but not charred. Leave then in the pan to cool, pop the cookie sheet in the freezer and then bag individually frozen figs.

UNEXPECTED COMPANY PORT SOAKED FIGS
The Boston Cooking-School Magazine, May 1905

"Steamed figs, served hot with cream, are a favorite dish at vegetarian and physical-culture restaurants. For a richer dish or preserve they may be simmered—the dried ones—in a rich syrup flavored with orange or lemon peel and some of the juice. When done, add a generous libation of wine, preferably Port. It keeps well and is convenient in winter, if one has not a supply of summer-made preserves to rely upon. Conveniently stored in the sideboard, it may come forth, when unexpected friends happen in for luncheon or a Sunday night supper, and will be sure to win praise. This is called by some Figs a la Genevieve."

Author's note: Figs do love Port. Soak some fresh figs overnight in Ruby Port along with a bay leaf and add to your favorite chicken fricassee recipe.

MONTH OF SEPTEMBER

Peach Dumplings

P LACE plenty of fresh milk on the inside of any two-year-old girl or boy. Add early bed-time hours and day-time naps; season with fresh air and sunshine; sweeten with smiles and kisses. Nature will round into the approved dumpling shape.

PEACHY CHOCOLATE UPSIDE DOWN CAKE
A Cook book for Victory, 1944

PEACHY CHOCOLATE UPSIDE DOWN 31.
CAKE.
Melt 3 Tbls. butter in 8 x 8 pan over low flame. Add 1/3 cup sugar and 1 1/2 tsp. grated orange rind and cook and stir until thoroughly mixed. Then arrange 1 1/2 cups sliced peaches, well drained. Decorate with almonds or walnuts if desired.

–Chocolate batter–
1 c. sifted swansdown flour
1/2 tsp. soda   1/4 tsp. salt
2/3 c sugar   4 Tbls. shortening or
1 egg well beaten   butter
6 Tbls. milk   1/2 tsp. vanilla
         1 square unsweetened choc. melted.
Sift flour once, and measure, add soda, salt, sugar and sift together 3 times. Combine butter, beaten egg, milk and vanilla.   Add to dry ingredients and last add melted chocolate. Beat vigorously and spread over peaches. Bake about 45 min. at 350. Loosen cake from sides of pan and turn upside down on dish having peaches on top. Serve with or without whipped cream.
         Mrs. Theodore Hatje.

The Immanuel Woman's Club of Meriden, Connecticut, held a victory fund-raiser in 1944 and sewed together my tiny 46 page typed cookbook with a pasted magazine photo of a retro kitchen on the front. What a gem it is, and I wanted you to see the recipe page for yourself.

To make this cake, use 2 Tbs. brown sugar (in place of the one third cup sugar called for) with the butter and peaches, and add the orange rind to the chocolate cake. Fresh peaches are better than canned, and late-season peaches are extra good. Roasted peaches are fun as well (see page 63). Bake this cake in a buttered glass pie plate.

MONTH OF SEPTEMBER

> ## FALL FRUIT HONEYS
> *Chester County Recipes*, 19teens

Sugar-laden fruit honeys were popular from the turn of the 20th century into the teens. My tattered copy of Chester County Recipes contains three recipes for quince honey, one for pear honey, and one for French honey which is a British lemon curd. Make your quince, pear and apple honeys in September and October when the fruits are ripe, but serve them atop an oven-fresh biscuit on a blustery winter morning. Make curds during the winter citrus season.

Mazie's Pear Honey

"Grate 12 large pears, take 6 cups of water, 5 cups of sugar, 5 tablespoonfuls of vinegar. Boil all together until red or to desired thickness."

Katarine's Quince Honey

"Four quartered apples and 4 quartered quinces, 3 pounds sugar, 2 quarts of water. Simmer until consistency of honey."

Mary's French Honey

"Six eggs, 1 pound of sugar, ¼ pound of butter, juice of 4 lemons and the rind of 2 grated; mix well together, then cook until it becomes the consistency of honey. Place the vessel which contains it in another of water which will prevent it from burning."

LEMON, LIME, OR ORANGE CURD

¾ cup sugar	6 Tbs. butter, sliced
2 eggs	Juice and rind of 2 lemons

Combine sugar and eggs in a double boiler, add butter, lemon juice and half the rind. Stir until mixture is thick and a drizzle from your spoon leaves a trail on surface of curd. Press through fine mesh strainer and then add the remaining zest. Will keep refrigerated a couple weeks. Try lime or blood orange curd made the same way. If making gorgeous orange curd, add zest and juice from one orange and juice of one lemon. Blood oranges appear in markets in February. Curds are delicious on oat crackers, or spread on bread and then toasted.

BISCUITS

I teach a class called "Granny's Biscuits," and it's always full. Every-one who loves biscuits has a romantic notion of how they think a biscuit

ought to smell, feel, taste, and look. The ingre-dients you use will determine the outcome; but biscuits are just one of those things you need someone to show you how to make.

FLOUR

I'm walking into a hornet's nest with this one, be-cause biscuit bakers have strong opinions about flour. I prefer unbleached because I don't like to eat bleached products, but the bleaching process does contribute to biscuit tenderness. Those who live in the land of biscuits, a.k.a. the South, will tell you that you must use a soft winter wheat flour (which was at one time a southern crop). Any flour will do as long as it's White Lily. Sadly, White Lily recently defected from Tennessee to the Midwest after being bought by another bigger company. Don't you know that Southerners have their knickers in a twist about that one. However, they now make an unbleached self-rising flour that I'm happy with. I like self-rising flours because everything's already in there and it makes life easy. Check for sodium levels if you have concerns. Whether you use self-rising or regular all purpose flour, I always recommend organic flour if you can afford it.

SOUTHERN BUTTERMILK BISCUITS

2 cups self-rising flour	**¾ cup buttermilk**
5 Tbs. unsalted butter	**Pinch of baking soda**

Combine everything but milk in a yellow bowl. Mix the butter into the flour quickly so that it stays cold. I mix mine till crumbly, others say you should mix so that the butter is pea-size. Add enough milk to make a sticky dough that you can form into a ball. Knead it several times in all-purpose (not self-rising) flour. That's the hardest part, knowing how much milk to add. I like my dough soft. Now, dust well with flour and roll out 1 inch thick. Cut with a biscuit cutter straight down and place on buttered or parchment-covered cookie sheet. Bake in preheated 450º oven about 10 minutes until your biscuits look the way you think they should look.

BISCUITS

FAT

Lard was the traditional fat found in a biscuit in the 19th century and on farms where hogs were raised. When hydrogenated fats came along at the turn of the last century, that became the favored fat. These fats give biscuits that dense, biscuity texture many people love. Not me, I prefer to eat actual food, which hydrogenated fat products are not. So I use unsalted butter which gives a good flavor to biscuits, but butter creates a biscuit with a crunchy crust. If you don't like that, you can bake your biscuits so they're touching in the pan and they'll be softer. You might not be surprised to learn that vintage biscuit recipes called for much less fat than we use in modern biscuits. My recipes call for 5 Tbs. of fat to 2 cups of flour, but I only use 4 Tbs. Since biscuits are now "in," we're seeing recipes that try and make biscuits short as pie crust, calling for 8 Tbs. of fat per 2 cups of flour. You look at your tummy decide how much butter to use.

MILK

"Did you mention 'Biscuits' this morning?"

Buttermilk! For tenderness. A pinch of baking soda reacts with the acid in the buttermilk to give your biscuits an extra lift. If you don't have buttermilk, you can acidify your regular milk by adding a teaspoon of vinegar, but you can't fool me. If you want to use sweet milk, better listen to my friend, Johnny Otto's advice: "You *can knock a bull over with a skim milk biscuit!"*

CUTTING YOUR BISCUITS

Speaking of Mrs. Otto, biscuit queen, she was raised in the Smoky Mountains National Park near Gatlinburg, Tennessee, before it became a park in the 1930s. Not a soul on earth could out-biscuit her and I was lucky enough to steal some biscuit lessons before she passed away in 2000. She taught me to cut my biscuits straight down with a sharp edged biscuit cutter. If you twist, your biscuits will rise wonky.

ALMOST SOUTHERN BISCUITS

2 cups all purpose flour	**5 Tbs. unsalted butter**
2½ tsp. baking powder	**¾ cup buttermilk**
¾ tsp. salt	**Good pinch baking soda**

Sift together dry ingredients. Omit soda if using sweet milk. Follow directions for southern buttermilk biscuits.

SAUERKRAUT

TO MAKE SAUERKRAUT
The Home Cook Book, 1905

"Choose large cabbages with white heads, take off the outer leaves and shred the cabbages very fine. Lay the outer leaves round the sides and bottom of a cask or tub. Then put in the shredded cabbage in layers about three inches deep, sprinkling each layer with a handful of salt. Press down the layers and repeat the cabbage and salting till you have used your material. Then put on a layer of outer leaves, spread a cloth over the top and also a cover smaller than the top of the cask. Put a heavy weight on the cover—for instance, a perfectly clean stone. Set the cask in a warm place till the cabbage begins to ferment, then set it in a cool place. In making the change skim off the scum, wash the cloth, and wash or replace the outer leaves. Let the fermentation go on between two and three weeks. The sauerkraut is then ready for use." (1905)

Author's note: I make my sauerkraut in in this nifty Harsch crock. They are handmade in Germany and available online. The crock comes with stone weights that fit perfectly over the cabbage. The rim around the top is filled with water which prevents the formation of the harmless white scum that's formed during fermentation.

Library of Congress

SAUERKRAUT

SAUERKRAUT MADE IN A CROCK

The recipe on the facing page is a good one. Homemade sauerkraut is crunchy and light; you'll love it. Here's what to do if you don't want to make a barrel of kraut. Shred about 5 pounds of cored organic cabbage. Save the outer leaves. Toss cabbage with about 3-4 tablespoons of good sea salt. Use more salt in summer, less in cool weather. Into your very clean crock, layer the cabbage and pound as you go to release the juices. When you hear a squishy sound, add more cabbage. I tamp with the end of a rolling pin that's missing the handle on one side. When fully packed, cover with outer leaves and wipe down the sides really well. Cover the cabbage with a clean plate and weight it with either a water filled glass canning jar or gallon freezer bags filled with brine so that the cabbage is covered with liquid. Add 1 tablespoon salt dissolved in a pint of water if you need to. Cover with a plate and keep at room temperature one day, then move to a cool space for 2 weeks. Check after a few days and skim off white film that forms. Your sauerkraut will keep for months refrigerated.

THE FARM UP-TO-DATE
Farm and Home, October 15, 1916

Library of Congress

We have an automobile,
And electric everything,
Except the baby's cradle
And the children's garden swing.
Why, right in canning season
Mother is not cross a bit,
That 'lectric fan we bought her
Is the thing that made a hit.

A motor grinds the fodder,
Also separates the cream,
Then churns it into butter
Just like my grand-dad's dream.
It does the family sewing,
All the laundry work as well,
It runs the vacuum sweeper,
And rings the dinner bell.

It slices ham and bacon.
Likewise cabbage for the kraut,
That handy little motor
We could not live without.
I'd rather be a farmer
In these days of modern toil
Than the president of the steel trust
Or king of gas and oil.

~E.L. Reid

MONTH OF OCTOBER

t's early October and my daughter, Rita, and I drive past a loaded abandoned pear tree on the side of a city road en route to the local food co-op. Slamming on brakes, we jump from the car, recycled shopping bags in hand, poised to pilfer. Drat, the fruit's too high. "You're going to have to park under the tree, mom, and climb on the roof of the car to reach the pears." Well, you can't scare me. So up I go to pluck and toss the pears into Rita's bag below with the occasional tumble of hard fruit onto her pretty head. Small price to pay, a few bruises (Rita might argue that) and hoots from passersby, for the prized fruits that will grace the caramelized fall pear tart at our dinner table soon enough.

Boo! says Rita

October's the time to lay in the provisions for the coming winter before the first hard freeze. Greens are abundant, and root crops such as beets, turnips, potatoes, sweet potatoes, rutabagas, carrots, and parsnips are piled high on local farm market tables. In addition to late pears and apples, pumpkins and winter squash of every sort and size are waiting to be transformed into pies, soup tureens and ravioli stuffing. Why, let's have a harvest supper tonight!

OCTOBER

AN OUTDOOR FEAST

An Outdoor Feast in the Autumn Glow
Is better than other feasts, I know,—
For oh, the fire that you help to make,
Sends incense up for its builder's sake!
And you'll find no food on earth so good
As the food you cook in an Autumn wood!

HALLOWEEN LIBATIONS
I Go A-Marketing, 1900

"To be sure, I went a-marketing t'other day, and I was able to collect a stock of valuable information which I came home prepared to dish up for the delectation of any who chose to read and profit by it. But by some chance, or mischance, it occurred to me that All-Hallows Eve is near at hand, and that when it comes, you girls will be up to all sorts of pranks. Now, years and years ago I was a girl my-self, and I can dimly recall that the playing of pranks on the fairies' anniversary night induced a desire for liquid refreshment, either for the purpose of chirking up one's spirits when the omens proved unfavorable or for helping out the general merry-making when the signs foretold bliss." (1900)

Claret Tipple

"And a drink that seemed to me at that time apropos of either event we used to make by slicing half a dozen juicy apples and three lemons as a starting point. Then we would lay them alternately in a large bowl, sprinkling each layer plentifully with sugar, and over all would pour a quart of claret. Then we would let it stand for fully six hours, pour it through a muslin bag, and it was ready for use." (1900)

Cider Punch

"If you really long for drinks which seem suitable for the saddest days of the year, why then see to it that your cider jug is filled with sweet cider as a prerequisite, and go ahead. Call your first effort a cider punch. Peel a lemon and pour half a pint of sherry on the peeling; to the juice of the lemon add a cupful of sugar, a little grated nutmeg and a quart of cider. Mix this together thoroughly and then add to it the rind of the lemon and the sherry. Let it get perfectly cold on the ice, or if you are short of time, ice it when serving. Now if you wish to make this punch a bit more insidious you can easily do so by adding to it a wineglass of brandy. It will be quite as palatable also, I think you will find." (1900)

MONTH OF OCTOBER

HEIRLOOM BEAN SOUP IN A PUMPKIN TUREEN

Choose an old-time variety of pumpkin, keeping in mind the size you'll need for the amount of soup you want to prepare. Long Island Cheese, warty sugar and blue pumpkins all make good soup tureens. Cut the top off the pumpkin and set aside. Gut and scoop out stringy mass, saving the seeds to either dry and plant or, if they aren't too tough, you can toast and salt them for your soup topping. Turn the pumpkin upside down in a rimmed baking dish and bake at 350º until almost tender. Now, flip it right-side up and, place it in a cast iron skillet or other round baking dish that hugs the sides of the pumpkin. Pour your

cooked soup into the pumpkin, heat about 15 more minutes in the oven and when you set it on the supper table, your guests will gasp with joy! To serve, scoop a bit of pumpkin out along with the soup and top with roasted pumpkin seeds.

HEIRLOOM WHITE BEAN & SAUSAGE SOUP

1 cup dried beans	½ onion, chopped
1 cup chicken broth	2 cloves garlic
Italian sausage	1 stalk celery, sliced
1 carrot, sliced	Bay leaf and a twig of thyme
Handful thinly sliced kale	Salt and pepper to taste

Serves 4. Soak beans such as marrowfat, cannelini , yellow eye, or navy overnight. Next day, cover with an inch of water and simmer, lid on, until almost tender, about an hour. Slice as much sausage as you like and cook it in a skillet until browned, set aside. Sauté onion, garlic, onion, and celery a few minutes in extra virgin olive oil, then add to your soup pot with the beans, 1 cup bean cooking liquid, chicken broth, herbs and sausage. Simmer about 30 minutes. Add kale and water if too thick. Pour into the cooked pumpkin and bake another 15 minutes at 350º This makes a fine vegetarian soup; just omit the sausage. If you have great beans, you don't need added broth to season them.

MONTH OF OCTOBER

CAMPFIRE MEATLOAF IN AN ONION

Who doesn't love a caramelized onion cooked in the embers of campfire, fireplace or grill? Throw an unpeeled yellow storage-type onion in scattered embers at the fire's edge and after about 45 minutes, the outer burned layers can be removed to reveal smoky sweet innards to savor as-is or as a topping on fire-grilled crusty bread.

Another way to enjoy a baked onion is to stuff it with your favorite meatloaf recipe. To do this, you will cut through one side of the onion long-ways from tip to root-end, stopping halfway through at the innermost layer. Now, peel off the outer two layers and stuff with a couple tablespoons of your uncooked ground meat mixture. Continue with the next two layers of onion. You can get about three "sets" from one large onion. Wrap each in two layers of foil. Cook on active embers, turning every 10 minutes or so, for about 45 minutes. Let your guests unwrap their own packet at the table or fireside.

Filling options:

Any lean ground meat mixture makes a good filling ... beef, veal, pork, sausage (cook first or it will be too greasy), lamb, turkey. Cook to an internal temperature of 165º. If you have a vegetarian in your midst, stuff with roasted fall vegetables or even a crumbled and browned veggie burger.

Hunter-Trapper Fire

MOCK ANGEL FOOD CAKE
My Mom's *4-H Club Handbook,* 1930's

"Cut crust off a loaf of (unsliced) white bread. Cut bread into inch cubes. Dip cubes first into condensed milk, then into cocoanut. Toast over fire as you do marshmallows."

MONTH OF OCTOBER

MRS. WINKLE'S APPLE CATSUP
Farm and Home, October 15, 1916

I'm afraid to try this fascinating recipe, but I thought you might be less squeemish, so do let me know how it turns out.

"Pare and quarter 12 sound tart apples; stew till soft in as little water as possible, and force them through a sieve. To one quart apples, add one cup sugar, one teaspoon pepper, one teaspoon cloves, one teaspoon mustard, two teaspoons cinnamon and two medium-sized onions, chopped fine. Stir well, adding one tablespoon salt and one pint vinegar. Boil one hour and bottle while hot. Seal very tight."

FRIED GREEN TOMATOES

Pick tomatoes that are about to turn color, with a slight pinkish tinge to them, unless a frost is imminent, in which case, make do with whatever you have hanging on your vine. Top with fresh chow-chow pickle made from fall veggies, garlic mayonnaise, or just eat them as-is straight from your cast iron skillet.

Slice tomatoes into ½ inch slices, dip into thick buttermilk (regular milk will do) then roll in freshly ground cornmeal that's been seasoned with salt and pepper. Cook on medium heat in about a tablespoon of hot oil or butter until crunchy brown and fragrant.

To Preserve Carrots, Parsnips, and Beets all the Winter
The New Household Receipt Book, 1853

—A little before the frost sets in, draw your beets or parsnips out of the ground, and lay them in the house, burying their roots in sand to the neck of the plant, and ranging them one by another in a shelving position; then another bed of sand, and another of beets, and continue this order to the last. By pursuing this method, they will keep very fresh. When they are wanted for use, draw them as they stand, not out of the middle or sides.

MONTH OF OCTOBER

About every June and September, the bears come poking around our neighborhood which lies in a valley at the foot of the Blue Ridge Parkway national parkland. My uphill across-from-the-garden neighbor, Daniel, used to holler for me to take cover when he'd see a big

black bear lumbering my way as I weeded my garden, oblivious to the world. Over the years, we had many conversations about what to cook with the garden's bounty, but I always look forward to fall when I get to make Daniel's collard greens topped with chow-chow pickles. The sweet-sour tang of the pickled vegetables mates perfectly with the slow cooked earthy greens. Daniel passed away last summer, and I miss him as I plant this season's seeds. One thing's for sure, you have lots of time to ponder life and appreciate those you care for as you tend a garden.

FRESH FALL CHOW-CHOW

Also called "end of the garden" pickles in vintage cook books, you can make chow-chow about any way you like as long as you're not canning it. For that, you'll need to consult a canning guide with a recipe that is safe to water bath can. (See resources, page 146.)

Chop small:

1 red onion	1 green tomato
1 green bell pepper	Half a small head of cabbage
1 red bell pepper	

Toss with a mixture of lime juice or cider vinegar, a squirt of honey, a pinch of salt and a few mustard seeds. Let the flavors get acquainted in your fridge for a while, then spoon on fried green tomatoes or onto your hot collards.

Buckwheat Cakes, 1890

Buckwheat enjoyed great popularity in many parts of the country prior to the turn of the 20th century. If you happened to live in an area where it was grown, it's likely that buckwheat pancakes were an invited break-fast guest to your farmhouse about every winter morning. Just to be authentic, I figured I'd try this recipe out in the same sort of setting from whence it came. So I baked them up in our 1880s log cabin perched on the side of a mountain, far from electricity, plumbing and modern life. I mixed the batter by lamplight, let it sit overnight, then baked the pancakes up on the Home Comfort wood cookstove first thing in the morning. Wowee, they're good. Somewhere between a crepe and a pancake, these buckwheat cakes are best when made with freshly ground buckwheat (see resources, page 146), and drizzled with maple syrup.

1 cup water (filtered)	½ tsp. salt
1 cup milk (or water)	½ tsp. yeast
2 cups buckwheat (or use half all-purpose flour)	

The evening before you bake, mix above ingredients and let sit out overnight in a covered ceramic bowl. Next morning, combine the following and add to batter.

1 Tbs. molasses	1 Tbs. melted butter
¼ tsp. soda dissolved in ¼ cup water	

Bake on a hot, lightly buttered cast iron skillet.

Author's note: This recipe is an abbreviated version found in Sara Van Buren's, *Good-Living, A Practical Cookery-Book for Town and Country*. As was the custom in 1890, she suggests you "reserve 1 cupful of this batter as the foundation

Photo by Regina Cunningham

of the next batch of cakes. Leave it in the jar, cover it with a little cold water, and set it in a cool place until evening; then pour off the clear water from the top (if any); add the fresh buckwheat, water, and salt; stir smooth, and set away until next day, repeating this process as long as you care to eat buckwheat cakes." Instead, refrigerate the leftover batter up to a week and then start the process as above, but omit the yeast.

MONTH OF OCTOBER

HANNAH'S GREEN TOMATO PIE TIMBER

Bet you never heard of pie timber. It's canned pie filling. My Chester County Recipes book is just full of great "from scratch" recipes like this one that was contributed by Hannah M. Sharpless. The book was falling apart when I found it in an antique store booth, and now it's in even worse shape. I don't even know where Chester county is because the book has no cover, but the recipes contributed by various ladies with names like Mazie and Ida are from the 19teens. This recipe makes several quarts of canned pie filling. Hannah would have used one quart per pie.

"Seven pounds of green tomatoes, pare, slice and scald for a few minutes, drain off, then put three pounds of brown sugar, a small piece of ginger root and two sliced lemons. Cook until clear." (19teens)

GREEN TOMATO PIE

Here's a green tomato pie recipe based on Hannah's recipe above. Use green tomatoes that are close to maturity. This pie is not trying to be anything other than what it is. I think you'll like it.

2 unbaked pie crusts	Green tomatoes, about 4
½ cup brown sugar	A tart green apple
1 heaping Tbs. flour	Half a lemon
1 Tbs. thinly sliced candied ginger	

Thinly slice peeled apple and your green tomatoes. Mix sugar and flour and sprinkle half of it onto the bottom of your unbaked pie crust. Then, add a layer of tomatoes, one of apples, the ginger, and finish off with the tomatoes. Sprinkle remaining sugar mixture on top and squeeze the lemon juice about. Cover with a lattice crust and then give your crust a nice crimp. Bake in a preheated 400º oven for 15 minutes, reduce heat to 375º and bake about 30 minutes more until the pie is light brown and bubbly.

CRISPY DRIED APPLE SNACKS

There are a couple types of apple peeling gizmos like this 19th century model currently on the market. The less expensive one cuts thinner slices which can be easily dried into a delightful low-calorie crunchy snack. Just dip the slices into a bowl that contains ½ cup

Apple paring, coring and slicing machine.

water mixed with half a lemon and a drizzle of honey. Dehydrate at 140º overnight and store in a jar with a tight-fitting lid.

APPLE SHORTCAKE
The Rural Cook Book, 1907

"Butter thickly an oblong granite baking dish. Halve and core as many good cooking apples as will fit tightly in dish; sprinkle with half a teacupful of sugar, several grates of nutmeg and add three tablespoonfuls of boiling water. Make a rich shortcake dough and roll and cover the apples. Bake in a quick oven half an hour. Loosen round the edges of the crust, turn it upside down on a hot platter, with a heated knife cut into squares and serve at once." (1907)

Author's note: A shortcake is just a sweetened, rich biscuit dough. Add two extra tablespoons each of butter and sugar to buttermilk biscuits (page 86). Bake at 400º in lower third of oven until biscuits are browned and filling is bubbly.

LILLIAN!!!

"Lillian," said mother severely.

"There were two pieces of cake in the pantry this morning and now there is only one. How does this happen?"

"I don't know," replied Lillian regretfully. "It musta been so dark I didn't see the other piece."

~*Farm and Home*, Oct. 15, 1916

MONTH OF OCTOBER

APPLE BUTTER
Good Housekeeping, Nov. 1894

"Take sweet cider, on the day it comes from the press, boil it down one-half, and add slightly more than half the quantity of pared, cored and sliced apples. Cook slowly and carefully, stirring with a long wooden paddle which reaches the bottom of the kettle, and skimming when necessary. When the apple begins to break, sweeten to taste, but it is better if left quite tart. Continue the cooking and stirring till the apple becomes a homogenous mass like marmalade. It will keep for any length of time in stone jars or wooden vessels." (1894)

POOR MAN'S PIE
Aunt Mary's Cook Book, 1881

"Butter a pie plate; fill it with sliced apple, and put a crust over it. Bake it, and when done, turn it over on to another plate. Sprinkle on the apple a little sugar and nutmeg; serve hot." (1881)

APPLE PIE

6 cups apples, sliced
½ cup brown sugar
2 Tbs. flour
Cinnamon and nutmeg to taste
2 Tbs. orange marmalade

Toss above ingredients and place in pie plate lined with pie crust. Cover with top crust, crimp and vent it real pretty. Brush with cream or milk and sprinkle with sugar (not the edges). Chill for about 30 minutes while you heat the oven. Place in a 425º oven for 15 minutes, turn the heat down to 350º and continue baking until innards bubble.

MONTH OF NOVEMBER

THANKSGIVING BOUNTY

Thanksgiving is just about the only holiday in America where we gather at the table with family and friends to celebrate the harvest with foods that are indigenous to our country, or at least our continent. There's turkey, cranberries, sweet potatoes, corn, pumpkin, black walnuts , pecans and pie. I know, I know. We don't grow pie. But pie is ours, too. Pumpkin, apple, pear, pecan ... they're all in season right now.

TERKEY DINNER
The Housewife Magazine, November, 1905

"An eight-year-old lad was asked to write out what he considered a good dinner bill of fare, and here it is:"

FURST CORSE.
Mince Pie.
SEKOND CORSE.
Pumpkin Pie and Terkey.
THIRD CORSE.
Lemon Pie, Terkey, Cranberries.
FOURTH CORSE.
Custard Pie, Apple Pie, Mince Pie,
Chocolate Cake, Ice-cream and
Plum Pudding.
DESERT.
Pie

MONTH OF NOVEMBER

CRANBERRY WINE, 1915

From a handwritten recipe in the back of F.W. McNess' Cook Book circa 1915. Scrofula was the term for a tuberculosis infection of the lymph nodes most often in the neck. I'll stop there, it's not pretty. Believe me, you'd rather drink this wine than have scrofula!

"Mash ripe cranberries into a fine pulp. Put them into a stone jar adding one quart of water to every two quarts of berries. Stir well, set aside and let stand a week. Then strain through a cotton cloth and you have a beautiful wine. With a little sugar, it makes a cooling and palatable drink and will not ferment. It is a specific for scrofula."

Author's note: This wine won't ferment much because there's no sugar added.

CRANBERRY CORDIAL

I haven't tried the cranberry wine yet, but this cordial, I have. Make it in November and then serve it a month later. Makes a nice gift.

> **1 12 oz. package fresh cranberries, about 3 cups**
> **1 cup sugar (less or more to your taste)**
> **3 cups light rum**

Chop cranberries roughly (about in thirds), add sugar and let sit until the sugar is dissolved. Put them in a sterilized quart jar and add rum. Shake well. Let cordial sit until you remember it in 4 weeks or so. Strain out the cranberries and keep them in the fridge to add to your apple pies.

CRANBERRY JUICE
The Housewife Magazine, November, 1905

"Take one pint of cranberries, and add to them one quart of boiling water. Stew half and hour in a porcelain-lined or granite dish, then press and strain. Add to the juice one pound of granulated sugar, and let it come to a boil twenty minutes. This will be in the form of a thick syrup. Skim and bottle for use. Take a tablespoonful to a glass of water, and you have a delicious cooling drink, with just enough acid to it to greatly help the appetite." (1905)

Author's Note: A super-sweet syrup intended to be bottled; decrease sugar to your taste. Note that it's to be used only as a light flavoring for water or seltzer.

MONTH OF NOVEMBER

CREAM OF CELERY SOUP
Handwritten late-19th century cooking journal

Cream-of-Celery Soup.   *Hearth + H.*

When you wash a bunch of celery, taking the white, crisp pieces for use on the table without cooking, save all the outer stalks and leaves for soup. Cook for 3/4 of an hour in enough boiling salted water to cover; when tender, rub through a colander, add a quart of scalding milk, thickened with a tablespoon of each flour and butter, season to taste with pepper and salt, and serve with crackers.

SIMPLICITY SWEET CORN AND NUT BUTTER
Unfired Food, 1910

There's nary a nut in this nut butter recipe, and corn is not ripe at the same time as are cranberries; however, cranberry butter is a beautiful sight to behold, and makes a festive addition to your Thanksgiving table.

"Eat natural food to maintain and increase your physical and spiritual health and avoid all food which ensnares the appetite with artificial flavors and chemically changed consistency.

Lay in one dish a neat looking, fully grown 4 or 5 oz. young sweet corn ear and place beside it a butter chip with ½ oz. savory butter, horseradish butter, or cranberry butter." (1910)

CRANBERRY BUTTER

½ cup softened butter	½ cup chopped fresh cranberries
2 Tbs. confectioner's sugar	Grated rind of half an orange

Whip the butter, add the sugar and orange rind. Beat in finely chopped cranberries. It will keep, refrigerated, a couple weeks, stored in a glass jar. If you want a bright pink butter, make it in a food processor.

MONTH OF NOVEMBER

THE HOUSEWIFE

Scotch Oat Crackers

Scotch oat crackers are crisp and good as well as cheap. To make, take two cupfuls of rolled oats, a quarter cupful of milk, a quarter cupful of molasses, one and a half tablespoonfuls of fat, a quarter teaspoonful of soda, a teaspoonful of salt. Crush or grind the oats in the food-chopper and mix with the other ingredients. Roll out in a thin sheet and cut into squares. Bake for twenty minutes in a moderate oven.

CRUNCHY HEARTY OAT CAKE CRACKERS

The recipe above from How to do Things, 1919, is mighty close to the oat cakes I learned to make in England a few years back. I keep a tin of these rustic simple "biscuits" always on hand to enjoy as-is, or with a bit of good blue cheese crowned with a dab of homemade fig jam. They're also terrific topped with a bit of chevre or cream cheese, drizzled with dandelion honey.

1¼ cup rolled oats	**5 Tbs. cold cubed butter**
¾ cup all purpose flour	**1 Tbs. brown sugar, packed**
½ tsp. soda	**3-4 Tbs. milk or half and half**
½ tsp. salt	
Squirt of lemon juice or vinegar	

In a food processor, combine dry ingredients and pulse about 10 times with butter. Add the squirt of lemon juice or vinegar and then enough milk so the mixture holds together. On a board, knead a few times, then roll out thinly. Cut with a small round cutter or just cut into 2-inch squares and give each cracker a couple pokes with a fork. Place on parchment-lined baking sheet and bake at 375º about 12 minutes until lightly browned. Makes about 30.

Two Ways of Sausage Making

The *right* way is to use a machine that *cuts*. That's the Enterprise way. Easy running and thorough, even cutting, just as coarse or as fine as you want it. That means good sausage.

The **wrong** way is with a machine that grinds and crushes instead of cutting. That means hard, slow work, and stringy, uneven sausage. Make your sausage the right way with the Enterprise Meat and Food Chopper.

No. 10
$3.00

After sausage season, the chopper will be useful every day in the year for the preparation of other food.

Nothing can get by the four-bladed, revolving knife and pass through the perforated plate of an Enterprise Chopper without being actually *cut* — the cutting action is as positive as a pair of shears.

Sold by dealers in hardware and housefurnishings.

ENTERPRISE

MEAT AND FOOD CHOPPER

Be sure the name "Enterprise" is on the machine you buy.
Write for the "*Enterprising Housekeeper*," a book of 200 choice recipes. Tells you different ways to lighten labor with the Enterprise Food Choppers, Sausage Stuffers and other kitchen conveniences. Sent free.
THE ENTERPRISE MFG. CO. OF PA., 216 DAUPHIN STREET, PHILADELPHIA, PA.

HOME MADE SAUSAGES
Practical Recipes, 1909

I've been playing around with sausage-making lately. First I tried to resurrect Grandmother's Enterprise food chopper, but it's duller than doughnuts. So then I tried Aunt Mary's 1951 Dormeyer mixer grinder attachment. The only blade I have is the one to make her pimento cheese and you can't grind meat with that. The food processor will do, but a better option is to have your butcher grind you a pork shoulder or loin with a little fat. Add about ¾ teaspoon salt per pound.

"Cut good sized pieces from loin of pork, retaining all the fat. Put in grinder, season with summer savory, sage; more savory than sage, salt and pepper. Form in small pats and fry in an iron frying pan. If you prefer, you can put sausages on small wire platter, and put that in center of baking pan. Cut some apples in half and core them and lay in under pan, put in a little water. Bake in an even oven and the dripping from sausages will season the apples deliciously." (1909)

Author's note: Or, you can cook your apples separately, then add to the cooked sausage and throw in a few sliced, cooked sweet potatoes. Drizzle with a hint of maple syrup and sprinkle with pepper.

MONTH OF NOVEMBER

ROASTED KALE CRISPS

Who would ever guess that oven-dried kale would taste so very good? I happened upon this method quite by accident while roasting brussels sprout halves. The random single sprout leaves toast up a pale golden brown and have a nutty flavor. Amazingly, kale tastes just as good toasted. If you're trying to give up high calorie crunchy snacks, try these instead. You'll wonder what you ever saw in a chip.

Devein a half a bunch of dinosaur or curly kale and cut in half, lengthwise. Toss with a drizzle of olive oil, a little salt and a few red pepper flakes. Spread on a

Photo courtesy Library of Congress

cookie sheet and bake in a 250º oven for 25 to 30 minutes until dry but not browned. Now go off someplace by yourself to eat them so you don't have to share with anyone.

BAKED CORN
Practical Recipes, 1909

Just a homey corn pudding that's a welcome guest at your winter holiday table. It's also good baked in a whole red bell pepper during corn on the cob and pepper season.

"1 quart of tender corn cut from the cob, 1 pint of sweet milk, 1 table-spoon of butter, 2 eggs, salt to taste; beat all well together; put in a baking dish and bake slowly until done." (1909)

MONTH OF NOVEMBER

*P*erchance, have you tried the moist Boston brown bread that comes in a can? The round slices taste best slathered with cream cheese. Well, here's its grandma. Boston steamed bread is traditionally made from rye instead of graham flour and you can make that substitution in this recipe. You'll also use 2 cups of buttermilk instead of sweet milk and add 1 cup each of raisins and toasted walnuts.

Steaming is easy and produces an exceptionally moist loaf. To steam on the stovetop, butter about four wide-mouth pint jars and fill halfway with batter. Seal each with a piece of foil. Place the jars in a covered tall pot, on a rack to keep the jars off the bottom of the pan. I use my trusty metal canning jar lids. Fill pot with two inches of water and simmer, lid on, for about 1½-2 hours until the bread's a nice caramel color. You can also steam in the oven. For this method, divide the batter between two buttered loaf pans and cover with foil. Set pans in a large baking pan filled with one inch of water and bake for 1½ hrs.-2 hours in a 325° oven.

BOSTON BROWN BREAD
How to do Things, 1919

Boston Brown Bread

Boston brown bread is a good standby. To make it, use one cupful of white flour or bread-crumbs, one cupful of corn-meal, one cupful of Graham flour, one teaspoonful of salt, three-quarters of a cupful of molasses, one and three-quarter cupfuls of sweet milk, three-quarters of a teaspoonful of soda, one teaspoonful of baking-powder. Sift the dry ingredients together then stir them into the liquids. Fill well-greased cans two-thirds full, cover tightly and steam for four hours. Good either hot or cold.

MONTH OF NOVEMBER

MRS. PAINTER'S PUMPKIN PIE
The Art of Cooking in Salem, WV

Mrs. Painter's pumpkin pie just might be the best pie you'll ever eat for breakfast. If you're a real pie eater, you know that nothing beats a piece of pumpkin pie first thing in the morning with a cup of hot coffee. Born of an egg-shortage, this fabulous firm pie substitutes a tablespoon of flour for one of the eggs usually called for in a pumpkin pie. Canned, unspiced pumpkin will do in a pinch, but for Thanksgiving, how about using a local heirloom variety of winter squash? (Pumpkins are winter squash.) From the North Georgia mountains up to Western North Carolina and East Tennessee, we favor the Candy Roaster pumpkin. It's a giant orange/pink pumpkin with a firm, sweet flesh that will pony up about 6-10 pies apiece. Warty sugar pumpkins are prized for pies as are any of the blue varieties of winter squash.

1½ cups pumpkin purée	¾ cup brown sugar
1¼ cups evaporated milk	Pinch salt
1 egg	1 Tbs. flour
1 tsp. each cinnamon and ginger and a grating of nutmeg	

Mix all ingredients well and pour into an unbaked 9-inch pie shell. Bake in bottom third of preheated 400º oven for 10 minutes, then turn heat down to 350º and bake about 45 more minutes until set in the middle. Decorate top with pre-baked seasonal pastry cutouts after the pie comes out of the oven. Bake first thing in the morning and chill before serving.

HOW TO BAKE A PUMPKIN

Cut your heirloom pumpkin in half, gut and save seeds to plant. Place on a foil-covered baking sheet, cut side down. Bake at 350º for as long as it takes to soften. Scrape out pulp or just peel off the outer skin. Pulse pulp in the food processor a few times to prevent stringiness. You'll have extra, so measure out portions needed for your favorite pie recipe, and freeze in separate containers.

MAUDIE'S RUM APPLESAUCE FRUITCAKE

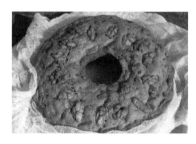

My teetotaling grandmother used to bake this cake at Thanksgiving in a big tube pan. There it would sit, wrapped in rum-soaked muslin that was re-doused weekly, until Christmas dinner. Just as the pumpkin pies were set out on the sideboard, out came the woozy cake to be served with a gen-erous dollop of hard sauce, and I mean hard sauce laced with so much rum that just one whiff would make you swimmy-headed. I suppose rum doesn't count as alcohol when it's in your food.

This fragrant fall harvest cake doesn't have all those bitter and scary colored fruits that make fruitcake the brunt of many a bad joke, though my grandmother did dot the top with red and green cherries for effect. I make my applesauce from Gold Rush apples, cooked without added sugar in just a splash of water, and I bake the cake in my grandmother's bundt cake pan with a row of pecans across the top for decoration.

1 cup unsalted butter, softened	1 cup raisins
¾ cup dark brown sugar	1 cup diced apricots
1 cup white sugar	1 cup sour dried cherries
3 eggs	1 cup chopped dates
Scant 2 cups warm applesauce	1 cup dried cranberries
3½ cup flour	Zest of an organic orange
½ tsp. salt	A little chopped candied ginger
2 tsp. soda	Golden rum
2 tsp. cinnamon	1 cup coarsely chopped pecans
1 tsp. ground ginger	

Pinch each of ground cloves and freshly ground nutmeg

The day before you bake, add about ½ cup rum to your dried, chopped fruit (minus the dates) and let sit in a covered glass container. Toss the fruit around in the liquid occasionally so it all soaks in.

Maudie's Rum Applesauce Fruitcake, continued ...

Preheat oven to 300º, grease and flour a tube or bundt pan and one metal bread pan as well. Cream butter and sugar, add eggs one at a time. Toss about ½ cup flour with the dried fruit and sift remaining dry ingredients. Add alternately with the applesauce and beat just until combined. Stir in the dried fruit with a big old worn out wooden spoon and blop into baking pans, about half full. Bake about an hour and 15 minutes until cake is golden brown and starts to pull away a tad from the pan sides.

When cool, swaddle cakes in unbleached cheesecloth that has been dipped in golden rum. Wrap the boozy cakes in parchment paper or several layers of waxed paper and keep in a closed tin until the December holidays. Re-douse the cheesecloth with rum when it dries out. Before serving, refrigerate the cake so that it holds its shape when sliced.

HARD SAUCE
Practical Recipes, 1909

"1 tablespoon butter, 2 tablespoons powdered sugar. Rub together thoroughly and then add nutmeg to taste and add a glass finest cognac."

MAKING "COOKEY MEN."

Saturday has come, again,
  And now I'll have some fun ;
Mother and I will cook-books take
  And to the kitchen run :
Cooking-aprons we will don,
  Hands will wash and, then,
We will spend an hour or two,
  Making " Cooky-men."

~*Good Housekeeping*, 1888

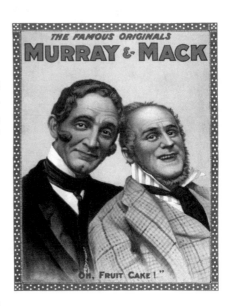

WINTER

Aren't you glad you put so much food by last summer? You've got your root cellar chock full of apples, pears, potatoes, winter squash, pumpkins, onions, pickles, sauerkraut, jam, fruit, tomatoes, beans, corn, soup and veggies. Now you have time to think about baking some bread.

BREAD-MAKING.

" Who hath not met with home-made bread,
A heavy compound of putty and lead ? "

—Thomas Hood.

Bread
The Kind Mother Used to Make

BREAD BAKING

"For good bread three things are essential: good flour, good yeast, and great care." Wouldn't the authors of my disintegrating and battered 1887 version of *Successful Housekeeping* be surprised to find that what held true in 1887 remains true today, some 120 years later. Bread baking is just what you need on this chilly winter morning, so get out your big yellow-ware bowl and let's get started.

I thought I'd stick to one really good vintage cook's advice and recipes for bread baking and for this I've chosen Mrs. Ida Bailey Allen. With a nickname like "The Nation's Homemaker," this 1920s radio cooking show host had 50 or so cookbooks to her credit as well as decades as a culinary columnist. I figure she ought to be able to tell us a thing or two about dough. Let's see what Mrs. Allen has to say on our three successful bread baking essentials from her 1917 book entitled, what else, *Mrs. Allen's Cook Book.*

First essential; good flour. *"When a real whole-wheat flour or meal can be obtained, one made of undenatured or unrobbed wheat, bread becomes a true nerve, blood, and bone food."*
OK, Ida, we'll choose fresh ground whole grain for our bread.

Second essential; good yeast. *"It's made up of minute plants, the success of the finished loaf depends on their proper growth. Just as you coddle your Boston fern, the yeast plants must be nurtured until they have grown sufficiently."* And now, Ida, we'll add coddled yeast to our unrobbed grains.

Third essential; great care. Not so easy as the first two essentials. This is where I suggest you read up on bread baking and find good bakers to teach you hands-on. The more you learn about baking a good loaf, the more there is to learn; so for now, let's don't get hung up on the particulars. In fact, let's skip the kneading process all together and use some decent flour and a long fermentation thanks to the hard work of your lovingly clucked-over yeasts.

BREAD BAKING

UNKNEADED OVER NIGHT GRAHAM BREAD
Mrs. Allen's Cook Book, 1917

Makes a delicious loaf of bread with a delicate crumb that pairs well with a mild cheese that lets the earthy molasses flavor sing. This bread would taste "flat" by today's standards because bakers used less salt in all their baked goods when this recipe was recorded. In general, one scant teaspoon salt per cup of liquid produces a good flavor and texture.

Two thirds compressed yeast cake dissolved in ½ cup tepid water
2 cupfuls scalded milk
2 tablespoonfuls butter or drippings
1 teaspoon salt
¼ cupful Barbados molasses
3 cupfuls graham meal
Bread flour

"Add the fat, molasses and salt to the milk. Cool until tepid, then add the yeast and the meal, beating thoroughly. Beat in bread flour until not quite thick enough to knead, cover and let stand to rise over night. In the morning cut (press) down, divide into two or three loaves, turn into well-oiled bread pans, smooth the top with a knife, and let stand till double in bulk. Bake an hour in a slow oven." (1917)

Author's Note: You'll have to make a few adjustments to update this recipe:

Use ¼ tsp. dry yeast, there's no need to scald pasteurized milk, use butter as your fat, double the salt to 2 tsp., add molasses made from sorghum if you can find it (not horrifying blackstrap molasses!) and use a coarse grind of whole wheat flour and unbleached bread flour.

Make as above, let it rise about 10 hours, but don't punch down. Butter two loaf pans and divide your dough in half. Throw a dusting of white flour on the dough and, gently, without pressing out all the air, form into two loaves. Place seam side down in your baking pan and let rise until doubled, 1½ to 2 hours. Place in a preheated 375º oven and after 10 minutes, turn the heat down to 350º. Continue baking about 30 minutes more until it's nicely browned and pulls away from the sides of the pan.

BREAD
BAKING

DUTCH OVEN UNKNEADED BREAD

No-knead breads are all the rage these days. Not so much for convenience, but because you can produce a stunning and tasty artisan style hearth bread with very little effort. I've been baking this bread for over 30 years in the embers of the fireplace. Good flour, a wet dough, a long fermentation and the right pan are key. You will need a 5-quart cast iron Dutch oven with a lid that can withstand high heat. I found mine at a yard sale.

About 4 cups unbleached bread flour (or part whole wheat)
1½ tsp. salt
A couple pinches of instant yeast (bread machine yeast)
1¾ cup filtered cold water

Start the process about 12-18 hours before you bake. Into a large bowl, measure out your flour and stir in the salt and yeast. Add the water and stir, stir, stir. The dough should be too wet to knead, but firm enough to form into a slack ball in your bowl. Cover and let it sit at least 10 hours. Next morning, stretch and fold

the dough from the outside in, all around the bowl. When dough is puffed back up, form it into a ball by stretching sides and pinching at the bottom. You may need to throw a dusting of flour on it to handle it. Don't pound the air out of your dough as you work. Now get a smooth surfaced kitchen towel, rub lots of flour into it, and put it in a bowl that's about twice the size of your dough. Place your dough in the towel-lined bowl, seam side down and let it rise until doubled.

Meanwhile, stick your cast iron Dutch oven, lid on, in a 425º oven for about 45 minutes. When dough has doubled, dump it into the HOT pan, put the lid on, and stick it back in the oven. Some dough will stick to the towel, just pry it off, adds character to your bread. Bake for 30 minutes, then remove lid and continue to bake until it's a nice golden brown. Have your wits about you when you make this bread, and get the little kids out of the kitchen! To bake with live fire, use a Dutch oven with recessed lid and feet. Preheat with coals and bake as above, keeping hot embers above and below the oven.

BREAD
BAKING

CORNMEAL MUFFINS RAISED WITH YEAST (6 HOURS)
Mrs. Allen's Cook Book, 1917

This recipe calls for home-ground cornmeal, I love it! In fact, double the cornmeal in this recipe, use 4 cups bread flour, 2 Tbs. butter, 2 teaspoons dry yeast, 1 cup milk, scant 2 tsp. salt and 2 Tbs. honey or molasses.

- 1 cupful home-ground cornmeal
- 5 cupfuls bread flour
- 2 tablespoonfuls bacon fat
- 1 cupful scalded and cooled milk
- 1 compressed yeast cake dissolved in 1 cupful tepid water
- ¾ teaspoonful salt
- 2 tablespoonfuls sugar (optional)

"Mix together the dry ingredients and rub in the shortening with the fingertips. Dissolve the yeast, add to the milk and stir into the first mixture. Beat well, cover and let rise till doubled. Then stir down, drop into well-oiled muffin pans, let rise till double in bulk and bake about thirty five minutes in a moderate oven. If to be started at night for breakfast, use half the quantity of yeast." (1917)

Home Made Bread

MONTH OF DECEMBER

The Plum Pudding

Come, bear the Christmas Pudding in,
Decked gaily out with holly,—
And let your laughter join the din!
Now isn't Christmas jolly?

~From *A Thousand Ways to Please a Family*
With Bettina's Best Recipes, 1922

Frankly, I think Bettina would be rather taken aback with the annual December holiday dinner event at our house. It starts off typical enough with friends and family of many faiths filling the house bearing gifts of winter casseroles, cranberry orange salad, hearth-baked breads, pies, and the like. The long tables, set with vintage tablecloths and dishware are piled high with the feast made by many hands as the family string band plays traditional mountain tunes by the fireside. We toast (and toast), give thanks and the feast begins.

But then as the evening wears on, we find the best way to wear off the mountains of food we've consumed is to play a few rounds of attack spoons. You know, the game where you try and get four of a kind and the first to do so, grabs a spoon. Since there's one less spoon than players, the one who does without gets an "s" on the way to spelling spoon, or spoonzaroonio if we're feeling magnanimous. Well, we get a mite carried away and often find ourselves being dragged across the table by the spoon we're going for. All in good fun, mind you, in the name of the gathering together of loved ones at the table.

A friendly game of mother-daughter attack spoons.

MONTH OF DECEMBER

MILK.

To Preserve Milk—Colonial Fashion.—Provide bottles, which must be quite clean, sweet and dry. Draw the milk from the cow into the bottles, and as they are filled immediately cork them well up, and wire them on firmly. Then put a bed of straw at the bottom of a boiler, on which place the bottles, with straw between them. Fill up with cold water, heat the water just up to the boiling point, draw the fire, and leave it to get cold. Take out the bottles, pack them in sawdust in boxes, and store in the coolest part of the building. Milk preserved in this way is said to keep sweet and good over twelve months. *Good Housekeeping*, 1890

CRACKLY CHEESE STICKS
The Country Home, May, 1934

"One cup of flour, one cup of grated cheese, made in America, the kind my general store and yours keeps, a half teaspoon of salt, half of paprika, a speck of cayenne, four tablespoons of butter, a quarter cup of cold water, one-half teaspoon of baking powder. Sift all the dry ingredients together. Add the grated cheese and work in the butter with the tips of fingers. Add just enough cold water to make a stiff dough. Roll out and cut into narrow strips the size of a small lead pencil. Bake these in a very hot oven at 450 degrees about fifteen minutes." (1934)

Author's note: Irresistible! Use sharp cheddar, scant ½ tsp. salt, and, if you have it, ¼ tsp. each smoked paprika and dried chipotle pepper. Cut with a fluted pastry cutter. Bake for 8 minutes in a 425° oven. Best served hot.

Farm Journal, 1879: Always add a line or two on the margin of a letter to a lady. You can't imagine how much satisfaction a woman obtains in turning a letter upside down to read a postscript.

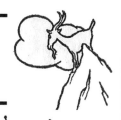

MONTH OF DECEMBER

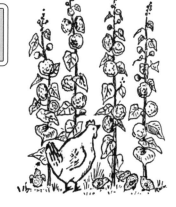

PHEASANTS ROASTED
Woman's Farm Journal, December, 1906

"Dress, lard, rub with salt, wrap in grape leaves, and roast from one hour to an hour and a half, in plenty of butter."

To Lard a Bird, 1872

"Cut fat salt pork into thin, narrow slices, and put one end of the slice through the eye of a larding needle. (You can obtain one at any kitchen furnishing store.) Now run the needle under the skin of the bird, and draw the pork half way through, having the pieces about an inch apart."   *~Appledore Cook Book, 1872*

Pin Feathers

~You can tell the age of a hen by the teeth; not hers, but yours.

~If you don't take care of your chickens, you needn't be particular about the breed.

~Cut bone will make the chickens laugh and lay, but if you are going to buy a bone mill, see that it is one you can run without the aid of a 4-horse engine.

Chicken With a Human Face
American Agriculturist, 1848

CHICKEN WITH A HUMAN FACE.—We have heard, says the New Orleans Delta, a good deal of talk during the last few days about a chicken with a human face, at the house of Madame Martin, in Cole street, near St. Philip. We paid no attention to the droll stories which we heard, but at length we were so pressed that we determined to see for ourselves. At the place mentioned, we saw a chicken, having, instead of a beak, a nose and mouth exactly conformable to those of a human face; the nostrils, the separating cartilage, the lips, tongue, chin, are all there. It was indeed a most singular *lusus naturæ*.

CHEWING GUM
Needlework Guild, 1906

"Prepared balsam of tulu, 2 ounces; refined sugar, 1 ounce; oatmeal, 3 ounces. Soak the gum in water, then mix all the ingredients; roll in powdered sugar to make the sticks."

Chewing a wad of gum is not necessary,

while chewing a cud *is*.

Everyday Manners for American Boys & Girls, 1922

"Never chew gum in cars or in other public places. A mild-eyed cow, standing knee-deep in lush grass and placidly chewing her cud, is a more or less peaceful addition to a pastoral landscape. Not so the school girl or boy feverishly chewing a big wad of gum, and talking and gesticulating at the same time. If you must chew, let it be within the four walls of your own particular room."

Death by Gum: *"The habit of chewing gum is like applying small air-pumps to the bases of the teeth. When the gum is separated from the teeth, it forms a vacuum between itself and the teeth, and the consequence is a violent strain on the dental nerves. This is bad enough, but when from sickness or other causes the habit must be discontinued, the result may be, and no doubt has been, fatal."* ~*Southern Field & Fireside,* 1860

HOUSE POISON

If the condensed breath collected on the cool window panes of a room where a number of persons have been assembled be burned, a smell as of singed hair will show the presence of organic matter; and if the condensed breath be allowed to remain on the windows for a few days, it will be found on examination by a microscope, that it is alive with animalcules. The inhalation of air containing such putrescent matter causes untold complaints which might be avoided by a circulation of fresh air.—*Philadelphia Bulletin.*

~*Good Housekeeping,* June 1888

MONTH OF DECEMBER

A PLAINER CHRISTMAS PLUM CAKE
Good Housekeeping, December, 1887

"One pound of flour, one-half pound of sultana raisins, one pound of currants, four ounces of citron, the grated rind of two oranges, one-half cupful of sweet, strong cider or wine, one-fourth pound of butter and the same of lard, four eggs, two teaspoonfuls of baking-powder, two of ground cinnamon, one of cloves, two of ginger, and half a nutmeg. Beat the sugar and butter to a cream, add the eggs, one by one; sift in the flour, warmed, and use only milk enough to make it a very stiff batter—almost a dough. Begin with a small cupful, add the cider, and then, if too stiff to pour slowly, add a *little* more milk; stir in the fruit last. Bake in two paper-lined pans an hour and a half."

"It is a blessing that we can stir up a little sweetness for ourselves when life neglects to send it ready-made."

CRISP AS GLASS GINGER SNAPS
Practical Recipes, 1909

"1 cup of New Orleans molasses; 1 cup brown sugar; 1 cup butter. Set the molasses and sugar over the fire and let it come just to the boiling point; then pour into the butter and add one tablespoon of vinegar, 1 teaspoon each of cloves, cinnamon and nutmeg. When perfectly cold add the flour into which has been sifted 1 teaspoon baking powder. Have dough stiff enough to handle, roll out as thin as paper and bake in a quick oven. They will be as crisp as glass." (1909)

Author's note: Crisp as glass maybe, but where's the ginger? A good recipe that deserves some tweaking. Replace cloves with 1 tsp. ginger and add only a pinch of nutmeg. Add ½ tsp. baking soda along with the baking powder to a cup of flour and mix that well with wet ingredients. Blend in about 3½ cups flour and roll into 2 logs. Cover with waxed paper and chill. Slice thinly and bake in a 325º oven until lightly browned. They burn quickly!

MONTH OF DECEMBER

VANILLA COCOA LOTION BAR

A solid lotion bar that will soothe your dry skin while leaving you with the alluring scent of chocolate pudding cake. OK, maybe not quite that dramatic, but close. It's best if you weigh the ingredients. You can find both beeswax and cocoa butter in one ounce portions at your local organic market. Vanilla beans are pricey, so I use only the hull after scraping out the seeds to use in my next baking. You'll need molds. I like to use decorative silicon muffin pans. Store the bars in those little round candy tins you can't bear to throw out.

3 oz. sunflower oil	**1 oz. cocoa butter**
½ vanilla bean	**1 oz. beeswax**

Warm the oil in a double boiler until you see ripples on the surface. Remove from heat and add vanilla bean. Let it infuse in the oil at least 30 minutes. Add cocoa butter and beeswax and melt slowly. Pour into molds. If you like a firmer or less firm bar, just remelt and add either a little more oil or beeswax. This will make about 5 bars.

Here are two other beauty product recipes to try from the July 1848 issue of *American Agriculturist* magazine. An earthen pipkin was a glazed redware pot with legs and a handle used in colonial era hearth cooking. If you'd like to try this cold cream recipe, use beeswax, organic coconut oil (in place of the spermaceti), and sweet almond oil. Let these ingredients cool, becoming semisolid before adding the rose water.

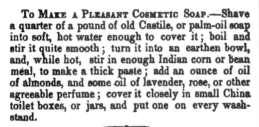

To MAKE A PLEASANT COSMETIC SOAP.—Shave a quarter of a pound of old Castile, or palm-oil soap into soft, hot water enough to cover it; boil and stir it quite smooth; turn it into an earthen bowl, and, while hot, stir in enough Indian corn or bean meal, to make a thick paste; add an ounce of oil of almonds, and some oil of lavender, rose, or other agreeable perfume; cover it closely in small China toilet boxes, or jars, and put one on every washstand.

To MAKE COLD CREAM.—Melt in an earthen pipkin, over a very gentle heat, a quarter of an ounce of white wax, and as much spermaceti; add, while hot, an ounce of the oil of sweet almonds; pour it into a bowl, and stir it until it becomes smooth and quite cold, adding gradually, drop by drop, a large table-spoonful of distilled rose or lavender water. This is particularly good for the hands, rendering the skin soft and pliant.

MONTH OF DECEMBER

THE PEANUT
The Peanut Plant, Its Cultivation and Uses, 1885

"It is safe then to say, that everybody likes them, and finds them palatable, healthful, and fattening. From a pig to a school boy, no diet will fatten sooner than roasted peanuts. A person can live on them alone for an indefinite period, if eaten regularly and with moderation. The analysis of the peanut shows it to be rich in the albuminoids, or flesh-forming elements. Roasted peanuts, therefore, form a very useful article of diet, and fill a place between the luxuries and the necessaries of common life. Wherever they have been once introduced, they cannot well be dispensed with; and as their use in this respect is constantly extending, this purpose alone would serve to keep the product before the public as a salable article. Once the peanut finds its way to the great cities of Europe, and roasted peanuts be sold upon the streets there, as well as here, the demand for them will far exceed the present limits, and the cultivation will be necessarily extended over a much wider area than now. There is every reason to believe that the demand for the crop will continue to increase."

PEANUT CHOCOLATE

"Peanut chocolate is made in some Southern families by beating the properly roasted nuts in a mortar with sugar, and flavoring with cinnamon or vanilla as may be desired. Peanut chocolate, is vastly superior to peanut coffee." (1885)

MONTH OF DECEMBER

READY RULE

This rule above all others heed:—
Have ready everything you need.

Before you start be sure to read
The whole receipt, then work with speed.

MOLASSES PEANUT BRITTLE
The Children's Friend, 1909

"To every half pint of shelled and blanched peanuts, use one cupful each of molasses and sugar. Boil the molasses and sugar together until the mixture is brittle when dropped in cold water; then stir in the half pint peanuts before taking from the fire. Pour into buttered pans and mark off into squares or lengths before it cools."

HONEY PEANUT BRITTLE
Gleanings in Bee Culture, December, 1940

Bee-licious. Really, this is a good recipe, the honey flavor is special, but honey absorbs moisture from the air, so keep this brittle in a glass canning jar. You only need to toast the peanuts if using raw. Use toasted and lightly salted Virginia peanuts if you can find them.

1½ cups peanuts, shelled	⅓ cup warm water
¼ tsp. salt	1½ Tbs. butter
1 cup sugar	½ tsp. vanilla
½ cup honey	½ tsp. baking soda (scant)

"Sprinkle nuts with the salt and warm in the oven. Combine sugar, honey and water in a large saucepan. Stir as it cooks, until it begins to thicken. Then wash down sides of the pan with a wet pastry brush, or with a clean, wet cloth wrapped around the tines of a fork. Cook without stirring until a few drops of the mixture forms very brittle threads when dropped in cold water. Add butter, flavoring and toasted peanuts. Stir in baking soda and pour quickly onto shallow buttered pan. Stretch out as thin as possible. When cold, break in pieces."

Author's note: Brittle threads are formed at about 300° (hard crack) on a candy thermometer.

MONTH OF DECEMBER

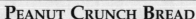

PEANUT CRUNCH BREAD
Handwritten Congoleum Flooring Cookbook, 1930s

2 cups flour	3 Tbs. fat
4 tsp. baking powder	¼ cup sugar
½ tsp. salt	2 well-beaten eggs
¾ cup milk	1 cup peanut crunch

"Combine all dry ingredients. Combine egg, milk and fat, add to dry ingredients. Stir in peanut crunch. Put in pans and let stand ½ hour before putting into oven. Bake at 350º about 45 minutes." (1930s)

Author's note: Baking powders are different now. Use half the amount of modern double acting baking powder. The cake must be baked right away instead of standing for ½ hour. The peanut crunch in this recipe was a store-bought brand of peanut brittle.

PEANUT BRITTLE CAKE

A variation of peanut crunch bread. When baked in an 8 x 8 inch cake pan, the brittle drops to the bottom of the cake forming a gooey sweet crunchy layer. Flip the cake over to serve.

1½ cups flour	½ cup brown sugar
2 tsp. baking powder	8 Tbs. softened butter
¼ tsp. salt	2 eggs
1 cup chopped peanut brittle	½ cup milk

Cream butter and sugar, beat in eggs one at a time. Add milk. Add wet mixture to sifted dry ingredients and stir just until mixed. Stir in brittle. Pour into a buttered cake pan. Bake at 350º about 50 minutes.

A Sign.—When you see a female rise early, get breakfast, and do up her mother's work in season, and then sit down to sew or knit, depend upon it, she will make a good wife.

THINGS YOU SHOULD KNOW

DEATH BY DISHCLOTH
Good Housekeeping, June 1888

WASH THE DISHCLOTH.

Now that diseases are known to be caused by germs, one is on the lookout for death in almost anything. Even a dishcloth may generate the germs that cause sickness and death. If it is black and stiff, and sour, throw it into the fire. Keep your dishcloth clean, if you have to eat without a tablecloth, do without curtains to your windows and cake for your tea, and have to let your face dry after washing it. Let the weeds grow in your garden, let the holes in the heels of your husband's or children's hose go undarned, let the shoes go without blacking for Sunday, if necessary, but do not neglect to wash the dishcloth.

A tidy housekeeper writes: "I have smelled a whole house full of typhoid fever in one dishcloth. I had some neighbors once—clever, good sort of folks. One autumn four of them were taken sick with the typhoid fever. The doctor ordered the vinegar barrels whitewashed, and threw about forty cents' worth of carbolic acid into the swill-pail department. I went into the kitchen and made gruel. I needed a dishcloth, looked around for one, and found several. And such rags! I burned them all, and called the daughter to get me a dishcloth. She looked around on the table. 'Why,' said she, 'there were about a dozen here this morning.' She looked in the wood-box, on the mantel-piece, and felt in the cupboard. 'Well,' I said, 'I saw some old, black, rotten rags lying around, and I burned them, for there is death in such dishcloths, and you must never use such again.' I took turns in nursing that family for weeks, and I believe those dirty dishcloths were the cause of all that hard work."

ABOUT SPONGES.
Woman's Farm Journal, December, 1906

"Sponges, unless they are properly cared for, soon become slimy and disagreeable to use, besides being unsanitary. Do not let it lie in soapy water. After each using, it should be thoroughly rinsed and squeezed and hung in the open air to dry, the sunshine if possible."

THINGS YOU SHOULD KNOW

HOW TO DO THINGS, 1919

From the folks at *Farm Journal Magazine* comes the book, *How To Do Things*. I can tell you that this gem of a book will teach you how to do just about anything you want to do. It's a masterpiece of repurposing. I'm about to go make a cup of coffee with my baking powder can percolator, but before I go, here's a small smattering of fun ideas.

Medicine Timer

This is made by cutting a piece of cardboard slightly larger than the top of a tumbler. Mark the figures, one to twelve, and opposite each hour mark cut a notch. Tie a knot in one end of a short piece of cord, pass it through the cardboard and fasten a button to the other end. When medicine is taken move the cord into the notch opposite the hour when it is to be taken again.

Fitting the Cork to the Bottle

Whittling a large cork down to make it fit a smaller medicine bottle is usually an unsatisfactory job. Here is a better way: Cut two clefts at right angles, as shown, and then you can neatly and easily force the cork into the small bottle. If properly done, the cork will fit into its place tightly and well. Try it.

Measuring Hard Butter

To measure butter without softening it: If half a cupful is needed, fill a cup half full of water, then add pieces of butter until the cup is full. If a cupful is wanted, repeat the process.

Simple Coffee Percolator

To make coffee for a small family the percolator shown in the drawing may be suspended in an ordinary coffee pot, with good results. A small baking powder can, a piece of wire, a center punch (or even a wire nail) and a hammer are the materials and tools required.

MONTH OF JANUARY

JANUARY

Simpler meals and wiser buying,——
More of planning,—less of hurry,——
More of smiling,—less of sighing,——
More of fun, and less of worry,
In this New Year's Resolution,
Trouble finds a swift solution.

ORANGE FENNEL SALAD

Fennel season will be here soon, and when it arrives, you'll be ready for this fresh, late-winter salad that's just the thing you crave after a couple months of hard eating. I learned to make this from an Italian olive grower whose family creates the most heavenly citrus-infused oils by pressing the rinds along with the oils. (See resource guide, page 146 for oil.)

Courtesy Library of Congress

On your prettiest flat individual salad plates, slice thinly peeled blood oranges (zest them first.) On top of the oranges, place paper-thin slices of fresh fennel bulb, tough core removed. Then a few thin slices of red onion. Over the top, drizzle a little orange-infused olive oil and a squeezing of fresh orange. A little chopped fennel frond on top and you're good to go. You can substitute good extra virgin olive oil and a sprinkling of orange zest for the infused oil.

MONTH OF JANUARY

RED CABBAGE SALAD
I Go A-Marketing, 1900

A really good cole slaw, actually. The salad dressing is homemade may-onnaise. Use raw eggs at your own risk; there's a small possibility of sal-monella infection (unless you're the one who gets sick, of course). The very young, old, and pregnant should avoid raw eggs altogether. When making mayonnaise, beat oil into other liquids drop by drop so that the mixture emulsifies. A saltspoon is just a couple pinches worth of salt.

"Before this you have probably made a red cabbage salad with a French dressing and with a spread of mayonnaise over it, so that you think you know it all, but have you tried adding to it some celery? This is the way it is done. All the coarse outside leaves of the cabbage are removed and the inside is finely shredded. Then the best stalks of a head of celery are cut into inch pieces and put into the salad bowl, a layer of celery, then one of the cabbage, and so on, heaping a bit in the centre. Garnish with the fresh green leaves of the celery; pour a dressing, made of a beaten egg, three tablespoonfuls of oil, two of vinegar, a saltspoon of salt, a dash of cayenne, and a suspicion of mustard, over all, and let stand for half an hour in a cool place before serving. For luncheon, when you are having croquettes of left-over ham bits, or of cold tongue scraps, this goes very near to being what would tempt any sane person to ask for a second helping." (1900)

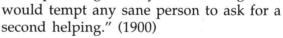

APPLE AND NUT SALAD
The Housekeeper's Apple Book, 1918

"Mix one pint of celery and one pint of apples cut into small matchlike pieces with one-half pint of English walnut meats bro-ken into small pieces. Dress with boiled salad dressing and serve in apple cups or on let-tuce leaves." (1918)

West End Bakery Carrot Ginger Soup

My friend, Cathy, serves this cheerful seasonal soup in her busy Asheville bakery. A steaming bowlful will warm your innards on even the chilliest winter evening. Don't let the lengthy list of ingredients scare you off, it only takes about 20 minutes to prepare.

4 c. water
1 sweet potato - peeled and diced, ½ apple - peeled and diced
1¼ pounds carrots - peeled and chopped (about 8)
½ onion - diced, 2 small stalks celery - diced, 1 Tbs. olive oil
A nice-size knob fresh ginger - peeled and grated
½ tsp. salt, or to taste
¼ tsp. cumin, ¼ tsp. corriander, pinch cinnamon
½ cup. cream, 1 Tbs. lemon juice

Bring water to a boil. Add carrots, apple and sweet potato. Meanwhile, sauté the celery and onion in the oil, then add to the soup. Cook until everything is tender, about 10-15 minutes. Add remaining ingredients and remove from heat. Using a stick blender, purée until smooth. If using a regular blender purée in batches. Serve with a little slice of Cathy's nasturtium butter (page 56) that you made and froze last summer.

Certain Rules of Health, 1907

Here are some certain rules of health;
Take them—they're better far than wealth :
Don't overeat, don't overdrink,
Don't overwork, don't overthink,
Be not afraid of honest sweat;
Run like a deer from shame and debt.
Beware of bigness of the head.
Get bigness of the soul instead.
　　　　　~The Rural Cook Book

Insert for a clever 1897 lamp stove. "It boils water in minutes."

MONTH OF JANUARY

The Faithful Hen

The gentle hen, black, red, or white, I love with all my heart.
She gives me eggs with all her might to eat or take to mart.

She never loafs, or sulks, or strikes, she's up at early morn.
She thanks me with her song, she likes, her wheat and oats and corn.

She wanders scratching here and there to find a bug or seed;
And be the weather foul or fair, her song's still heard, indeed.

And when, at last, her race is run, and her last egg we've got,
We still enjoy her, if well done, in roaster, pan, or pot!

PAPRIKA CHICKEN
The Rural-New Yorker Cook Book, 1907

"This is a favorite Hungarian dish. Cut a nice tender chicken into pieces as for a fricassee; flatten a little, such pieces as need it. Season each piece with salt and pepper, and dredge it lightly with flour, while you fry a minced onion in two tablespoonfuls of butter. Lay the chicken in the butter and onion, cooking for 30 minutes, so it will be evenly and thoroughly done. Take up the chicken and stir in an even teaspoonful of salt and a very scant teaspoonful of paprika, or half a scant teaspoonful of good mild cayenne pepper of any kind. Add last of all a cupful of rich cream. Make some dumplings of a pint of sifted flour, two teaspoonfuls of baking powder, a saltspoonful of salt and butter the size of half an egg; moisten the dumplings with a cupful of milk, and drop them over the sauce. Let them cook well, covered for 50 minutes, when they will be well puffed up and light. Pour the sauce around the chicken and make a circle of the dumplings. If the dumplings are steamed over the cream sauce so they do not sink into it they will be lighter." (1907)

MONTH OF JANUARY

Known both as an eccentric and one of the most influential scientists of the modern age, Croatian-born Nikola Tesla's turn-of-the-20th century electrical inventions would forever change life in the kitchen, and the world as well. No historic cookbook of this sort would be complete without a tribute to the man who brought us AC electricity, fluorescent lighting, robotics, radio, wireless electricity, and more.

Pi Pie

Here's a man who, in 1886, is digging ditches to keep from starving while figuring out how to create an X-ray tube in his spare time. In 1888, Tesla goes to work with Westinghouse Electric to develop applications for AC electricity over long distances. Meanwhile, in 1891, he develops his infamous Tesla coil, a device that wirelessly transmits electrical energy. Think about that for a moment as you plug in your desk lamp. Mind you, I wouldn't have given any of this much thought had I not produced a physicist offspring who replicated a Tesla coil himself just for the fun of it. Pretty much, you turn off the lights, plug this thing in and there's a loud drone followed by the sharp odor of ozone, brilliant arcs of light flying about, and then all the lightbulbs in the room light up by themselves as if by magic. And somehow, because of this gizmo's ingenious inventor, we, without a second thought, retrieve cold things out of the refrigerator, heat them up in the oven while listening to our favorite tunes on the radio.

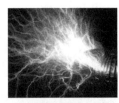

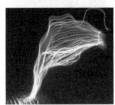

Tesla's Tesla coil

Wes' Tesla coil

MONTH OF JANUARY

MOVING PICTURE DISH, 1917

This recipe is from a WWI-era handwritten cookbook, clipped from Today's Housewife Magazine. Why is this a moving picture dish? Hmmm ... maybe it's an easy casserole to have in the oven waiting for you when you get home from the movies. Definitely a war-era recipe, peanuts reside where ground meat once dwelled. I double-dare you to try it.

"1 cup ground peanuts, 1 cup strained tomatoes, 1 cup cooked rice, 1 cup bread crumbs, salt, pepper. Mix all together and steam one hour. Sprinkle with crumbs and brown in the oven. This can be served either as a loaf or in a casserole."

The Dreaded Catarrh

The Peruna Almanac, A Handy Book of Information for the Family, 1905

A national disease, Catarrh, hovers ominously over every city, and nestles treacherously in every hamlet. It flies with vampire wings from country to country and casts a black shadow of despair over all lands. Its stealthy approach and its lingering stay makes it a dread to the physician and a pest to the patient.

I don't see as much of my husband as I used to.
Is he traveling?
No, he's been taking anti-fat. ~*Chicago News*, 1907

MONTH OF JANUARY

EGGS IN POTATO NESTS
Farm and Home, Annual Poultry Issue, February, 1918

"Left-over potatoes may be used for this dish. Shape the mashed potato into small nests, using about half cup of potato for each nest. Put a small bit of butter in each nest, then break in an egg, being careful to keep the yolk whole. Sprinkle salt and pepper on top and set in the oven until the egg is cooked and the potato slightly browned. Serve hot with crisp slices of fried bacon." (1918)

Author's note: Bake in a 350º oven.

AUNT MARY'S POTATO PUFF ROLLS
1930s Handwritten Cookbook

A soft, light, potato-y roll with lots of flavor, especially if you use leftover seasoned mashed potatoes. These will makes a good sandwich or companion for a hearty meat stew. Yeast and flour have been adapted for the modern cook.

Make a sponge of:

1 cup mashed potatoes	**1 cup milk**
2 tsp. active dry yeast	**2 cups flour**

Stir well. Let "work" for about 4 hours, then add:

1½ tsp. salt	**1 egg**
4 Tbs. unsalted butter, softened	**2 Tbs. honey**
Flour to make a soft dough (bread flour)	

Knead till smooth. Let rise an hour or two until doubled. Pat out into a rectangle about an inch and a half thick onto a floured board and cut all the edges with a sharp knife into shape you want. (Each roll should have 4 cut sides). Dust with flour and let rise on baking sheet until doubled, about 90 minutes. Bake at 375º until lightly browned.

MONTH OF JANUARY

DUTCH APPLE CAKE BREAD
Encyclopedia of Practical Horticulture, 1914

What fun it is to find a bread recipe from 1914 that needs almost no tweaking to bring it up-to-date. Here's an enriched bread with an ample apple topping that's just right with a cup of coffee. Our tasters squealed with delight when they laid eyes on this impressive fragrant artsy loaf.

"Mix one cup of scalded milk, one-third of a cup of butter, one-third of a cup of sugar and one-half a teaspoon of salt. When lukewarm add one yeast cake, broken into small pieces, two unbeaten eggs and flour to make a soft dough. Beat thoroughly, cover and let rise until the mixture has doubled its bulk. Beat thoroughly and again let rise. Spread as thinly as possible in a well-buttered dripping pan, brush over with melted butter. Press sliced apples into the dough in even rows. Sprinkle with one-fourth cup of sugar mixed with one-half teaspoon of cinnamon, then with two tablespoons of well-washed currants. Cover and let rise; bake in a moderate oven for 30 minutes. Cut in squares and serve plain, or with whipped cream."

Author's note: Follow the directions above with these changes. You don't need to scald pasteurized milk, but do warm it. Add the butter, melted, and increase salt to 1 teaspoon. Some grated lemon rind is a nice addition. You can use either one or two eggs, and you'll add 4-5 cups of unbleached all purpose flour. Knead as usual and set in a bowl to rise until doubled, about 2 hours. Spread the dough out on a sheet of parchment in a rimmed baking sheet. Press in about 4 peeled and sliced tart apples and sprinkle with the sugar mixture. Omit currants, they'll burn on top, but you can add them when you mix your dough. After second rise, bake about 25 minutes at 350º, until nicely browned. You can glaze the apples with some orange marmalade before or after baking if you like.

GINGERBREAD PEAR UPSIDE DOWN CAKE

A last-minute company-worthy dish, you can also make this in a cast iron Dutch oven in your fireplace. You can use just about any fresh fruit in season on the bottom. This makes one 8 x 8 pan or two shallow pie plates.

2 cups flour	⅓ cup butter
2 tsp. baking powder	⅓ cup sugar
¼ tsp. baking soda	⅔ cup molasses
½ tsp. salt	¾ cup buttermilk
1 tsp. cinnamon	1 egg
2 tsp. ground ginger	3 firm pears, peeled and sliced

A handful dried or fresh cranberries

If using dried cranberries, soak them in a little warm rum until plumped. Sift flour, baking powder, soda, salt, and spices and set aside. Cream butter and add sugar gradually, beating until fluffy. Add egg and molasses, then flour alternately with buttermilk. Beat just until smooth. Meanwhile, melt a tablespoon or two of butter in a skillet. Put 2-4 tablespoons brown sugar in the pan and let it bubble. Add the pears and toss until they're coated and sugar mixture is melted. Put the cranberries in the skillet, along with the pears and then pour the gingerbread batter on top. Bake in a 350º oven about 30-50 minutes until done. Carefully flip onto a plate soon as it comes out of the oven.

"Here's Chocolate Gingerbread

NEW (CHOCOLATE) GINGERBREAD
American Cookery Magazine, 1919

Stir 2 squares unsweetened Bakers chocolate, melted, into the above cake batter and bake in a glass 8 x 8 baking dish omitting the fruit.

MONTH OF JANUARY

Mrs. Martinson's Carrot Pie
McNess' Cook Book, 1920

1½ cups cooked carrots, mashed 1 teaspoon cinnamon
1 cup sugar 1 teaspoon ginger
1½ cups milk Pinch salt

Bake in open crust with whipped cream on top.

Author's note: Purée cooked carrots, use evaporated or whole milk, add a beaten egg and a tablespoon of flour so that the filling sets. Pour into unbaked pie shell. Place in bottom third of 400º oven and turn down to 350º after 10 minutes. Bake 45 minutes or until no longer wobbly in the center.

Orange or Lemon Extract
Needlework Guild Cook Book, 1906

"Select 6 nice oranges with oily skins and peel the rind very thin, avoiding any of the white part. Add the peel to 1 pint of alcohol. Let stand 4 or 5 days and then strain and it will keep an indefinite time. Lemon extract can be prepared in the same way."

Author's note: Use organic fruit, and if you can't get grain alcohol where you live, use 100 proof vodka. What the heck, if you don't feel like making orange or lemon extract, add sugar and you have an Italian limoncello.

Limoncello

8 organic lemons 3 cups water
750 m. bottle of 100 proof vodka or grain alcohol
2 cups sugar (You can use less)

Infuse the lemon peels (use a potato peeler to obtain yellow part only) in the vodka for 8 days, shaking bottle once a day, then strain. Heat sugar and water until sugar dissolves. Let it cool, then add to the lemon vodka. Wait 30 days before drinking. This is a really sweet after-dinner drink that packs an alcoholic punch. Orange liqueur (arancello) is made the same way.

MONTH OF FEBRUARY

February's Bounty

wouldn't call it bounty, really. More like summer's bounty stored for the winter. Even then, potatoes are getting squishy, your butternut squash are turning black. It's not pretty, but there are a number of good foods available at the market this quiet month that don't come from too far away. There's citrus of all kinds, greens, root veggies, watercress and fennel. February is a month of hunkering down and indulging in some good old home-cooked, soul-warming comfort food. Speaking of warming and comfort ... love is in the air. Happy Valentines Day!

Cookery Versus Poetry
American Cookery, May, 1919

I sought to lure my lover's heart
By writing pretty verses;
I thought to use such wiles and art,
As long ago were Circe's.
My love, he nodded while I read
The rhymes I called a sonnet.
"It's very nice, my dear," he said,
When asked his judgment on it.
It stirred his ardor not at all;
Alas! My toil was wasted.
I cast aside the Muses' thrall,
With joy to kitchen hasted.
I saw I had no time to spare
In writing high-brow ballads;
A cooking manual now my care,
My compositions, salads.
I baked a cake with spice and sweet,
As light as angels' kisses.
My love, he ate, and, at my feet,
Asked me to be his Mrs.

MONTH OF FEBRUARY

MID-19TH-CENTURY BUTTER

"Method of making excellent butter from the milk of cows fed upon turnips.—Let the bowls, either lead or wood, be kept constantly clean, and well scalded with boiling water, before using. When the milk is brought into the dairy, to every eight quarts mix one quart of boiling water; then put up the milk into the bowls to stand for cream. By keeping strictly to this method, you will have, during the winter, constantly sweet and well-tasted butter from the milk of cows fed upon turnips." ~*The New Household Receipt-Book, 1853*

Curious Mode of Making Butter.—If I want butter only for my own breakfast, I lay a sheet of blotting paper upon a plate, and pour the cream upon it. In a short time the milk filters through, and the butter is formed. If I wish to expedite the operation, I turn the paper over gently upon the cream, and keep it in contact for a few moments, and then press upon it, and the butter is formed in less than two minutes. If you submit it to severe pressure by a screw press, it becomes as hard as when frozen. I cannot think but the simplicity of this mode of proceeding would be universally adopted, if any better material than blotting paper could be thought of for the filter—the paper adhering too firmly to the butter, and the finest muslin admitting the passage of the cream.—*Gardener's Chronicle.* American Agriculturist, October, 1848

HORSERADISH AND RAW BEET RELISH

Fresh horseradish root is best dug in spring, but you can make this whenever you can locate the roots. Speaking of roots, my father taught me to make this relish; both he and this dish are rooted in eastern European Jewish tradition. The rowdy neon-purple relish is lovely with any kind of fish. Try it on a cracker with smoked trout and watercress.

In a food processor, combine 1 cup of peeled and diced fresh horseradish root, a small peeled and diced raw beet, 2 to 4 Tbs. sherry vinegar, and a pinch of salt. Grind in food processor, but do NOT breathe in the burning fumes when you open the lid. After a few minutes, taste and adjust the vinegar to your liking. You can add a drizzle of honey, but the raw beets should offer enough sweetness.

MONTH OF FEBRUARY

JUGGED CHICKEN, 1907

These two meat recipes are from "The Rural Cook Book: Some Old Recipes and Many New Ones—being the Collected Wisdom of a Legion of Home Cooks Published by The Rural New-Yorker." A non-fussy cookbook for regular people who didn't have a housekeeper to attend to things like cooking, cleaning, and tending the children. Jugged chicken is a colonial-era "receipt."

"Cut the bird up as for a fricassee. To every pound, allow two heaping teaspoonfuls of flour, one scant teaspoonful of salt and one-quarter teaspoonful of pepper. Mix thoroughly and roll each piece of chicken in the mixture, then pack closely in a large bean-pot. Sprinkle in a tablespoonful of minced onion. Cover with boiling water and bake in a good oven until tender — from two to three hours. When done remove to a hot platter, thicken the liquor for gravy and serve in a boat." (1907)

Author's note: Brown the floured chicken on all sides in a little oil before putting in the pot. A cast-iron Dutch oven is good. Add chicken broth in place of water, decreasing salt, accordingly. Bake, covered, at 325º for about 2 hours.

BEEF STEW GOULASH, 1907

"Cut two leeks or onions, small-sized ones, into fine pieces, and fry them in hot butter till they are brown. Add one cupful of beef broth, a little salt, half a teaspoonful of paprika or red pepper, and half a teaspoonful of browned flour. Stir until smooth, then strain out lumps if necessary. Have ready one-half pound of raw steak, cut into quarter-inch squares. The better the steak, necessarily, the better the result will be, and therefore porterhouse is preferred. Toss the meat into a frying pan just long enough to cook the outside, then add the sauce. Add two warm boiled potatoes, cut into good-sized pieces, and let the pan remain on the back of the stove 15 minutes before serving."

MONTH OF FEBRUARY

ROAST PORK LOIN WITH APPLE ONION JAM

This comes out of the kitchen of my friend, Brookes. She and her husband eat something as good as this EVERY SINGLE DAY! I'm not kidding. And she fits this in between her container garden business, teaching horseback riding lessons, and running the farm. Light a fire, uncork the wine, and call up some friends for this easy-to-make homey winter dish.

To serve four, butterfly a 2 pound pork loin roast or better yet, ask your butcher to do it. You want the pork in a rectangular shape about an inch thick. Rub a little salt & pepper into the pork. Spread the apple onion jam over the meat, then roll up with the grain. Tie the pork roll in about 3 or 4 places with kitchen twine and place in a glass baking dish. Some of the filling will spill out onto the dish. Bake the roast in a preheated 350º oven for about an hour until the innards are 150º. The roast will continue to cook a bit when you take it out of the oven. You can baste with a glaze of Calvados, olive oil, balsamic vinegar and honey as the roast bakes.

APPLE ONION JAM

One medium onion, thinly sliced
A spoonful of olive oil
2 tart apples, chopped fine
¼ cup dark brown sugar
2 Tbs. balsamic vinegar
¼ cup Calvados (apple brandy)

Slowly sauté the onions in the olive oil until they begin to caramelize, about 15 minutes. Add the apples, brown sugar, and balsamic and continue to cook about 15 more minutes. Add Calvados and simmer a few more minutes until the mixture becomes thick enough to spread. Goes great with pork or chicken.

MONTH OF FEBRUARY

GRITS

Few foods level the economic comfort-food playing field likes grits. According to The Picayune Creole Cook Book, 1916, "Whether rich or poor, there are few Creole families in New Orleans who sit to breakfast without a good dish of grits." Traditionally, only Southerners understood grits, but now they're showing up in diners and fine restaurants all over the country. If you think you don't like them, it's probably because you haven't had good grits, freshly milled from heirloom dent corn and cooked long and slow. Good grits don't need anything but salt, pepper and butter. But you can make a fine meal of shrimp and grits, dress up your salad with grit croutons, and then there's my all-time favorite, pan-fried grits. The mill that sells your grits (see resources, pg. 146) will have a recipe that's adapted to their particular cut of corn, but in the meantime, here's the general idea.

Boil 3 cups water in a heavy-bottomed saucepan. Sprinkle in 1 cup coarse grits and simmer with the lid off, stirring for at least 5 minutes until they start to thicken. Turn heat to low and keep an eye on them, stirring here and there, cooking until grits are tender. Cooking time varies from 15 minutes to an hour. Add about ½ tsp. salt when half done and then salt and pepper to taste when finished. Make extra because you'll want to have some to pan-fry.

NANCY'S PAN-FRIED GRITS

When my mother got out her cast iron skillet, good things were about to happen in her kitchen. This is my favorite of all the great things she made. It's good for breakfast, but we often had it for dinner as a side dish.

Put your leftover grits in a buttered loaf pan and refrigerate overnight. Next day, plop them out on the counter and slice them about a half-inch thick. Heat up your skillet, put in a pat of butter to melt, and then add grit slices. Turn heat to medium-low. After 10-15 minutes, they should be brown and crunchy and allow you to give them a flip. Serve hot with salt and pepper, drizzled with maple syrup.

MONTH OF FEBRUARY

1930 CONGOLEUM CORNMEAL WAFFLES

One of my favorite cookbooks is a hefty Congoleum flooring cata-logue with handwritten and clipped recipes pasted all over most of the pages. It's a primer on 1930s kitchen flooring as well as cooking. Here's a crunchy, fun waffle that calls for soaking the cornmeal, which would have been necessary with the coarse grinds available earlier last century. Use stone-ground cornmeal if you can. Lemon zest and blueberries love corn-meal. Throw in a handful of dried or fresh small wild blueberries if you happen to have them.

1½ cups cornmeal	1 cup flour
1½ cups boiling water	3 tsp. baking powder
3 Tbs. butter	½ tsp. salt
2 eggs	½ tsp. soda
½ cup buttermilk	1 Tbs. sugar

"Place the cornmeal in a bowl, add the boiling water and stir until smooth. Add butter and stir until melted. Let stand until cool or cover and leave over-night. Separate the eggs, beat the yolks, and add to the mixture. Dissolve the soda in the buttermilk and stir into the batter. Add the dry ingredients, which have been sifted together. Stir until smooth and fold in the egg whites, beaten stiff. Bake on a hot waffle iron and serve at once." (1930s)

Author's note: Add extra liquid to the batter if needed so that it's thick, but pourable. My friend, Richard, tested this recipe and I'll just share his words with you: *"The waffles cooked to perfection in our electric waffle-maker, rising nicely. They had a comforting old-timey flavor, especially topped with the carrot conserve (see page 19) and a bit of maple syrup. We used Brinser's Best Yellow Roasted Corn Meal, something we picked up at a market in Pennsylvania. This may be one of our new favorite cornmeals, if for no other reason than phrases on the package like 'Takes less meal to stir up a Mush.'"* Brinser's Best Corn Meal has been manufactured since 1878. The Handler Company that makes it is located in Manheim, PA. See re-source guide, page 146, to locate some of this great meal for yourself.

MONTH OF FEBRUARY

GRAHAM CORN BREAD,
The Modern Priscilla, January 1917

"The following formula produces a delicious light, tender, flaky loaf with the corn flavor: Mix 1 cup of white flour with ½ cup, each, of graham and fine corn-meal, ½ teaspoon of salt, 2 of sugar, and a heaping one of baking-powder. Then mix to a very stiff batter with about 1 cup of sweet cream or sour cream into which has been well stirred ¼ level teaspoon of baking-soda. Beat hard and ¼ hour in a very moderate oven.

The secret of perfection in this bread is a batter, or rather dough, so thick it will not settle or spread of itself when put in the baking-pan. Do not smooth it with a spoon, but merely shape it into the corners of the pan, leaving it rough on top." (1917)

Author's note: Try the recipe below.

CRANBERRY LEMON CORNMEAL HARVEST BREAD

Here's a version of the above bread whose flavor will grab you by the collar and shout yeehaa! It's the perfect winter breakfast bread. Grind your own corn and wheat or buy a coarse-ground variety with the germ intact if you can.

¾ **cup whole wheat flour**	**2 eggs**
¾ **cup cornmeal**	½ **cup unsalted butter, melted**
1 cup all purpose flour	**1¼ cups buttermilk**
1 tsp. salt	½ **cup maple syrup**
1½ tsp. baking powder	**1 cup dried cranberries**
⅓ **cup sugar**	**1 cup chopped pecans or walnuts**

Preheat oven to 350º. Toast the nuts a few minutes until they're fragrant but not browned. Butter a 9 x 5 loaf pan and coat the insides with a couple spoonfuls of sugar. Stir the dry ingredients together, including the nuts and dried fruit. In another bowl, whisk the butter, eggs, buttermilk and syrup. Add wet ingredients to dry and stir just enough to blend. Pour into baking pan and bake about an hour. It's done when nicely browned and firm to the touch.

MONTH OF FEBRUARY

Look at this. Bettina clandestinely presents Bob with a Valentine's Day cake. Notice that her cupid buddy is holding a backup emergency pie in case hubby's in more of a pie mood. What a woman! If Bob were to present something he cooked to Bettina ... not that he would, mind you, 'cause he golfs while she bakes him pies ... he'd give her Pin Money Fudge. Oh, for heavens' sake, what am I thinking? He doesn't even have pin money. He works at the bank. It's Bettina who has to save her butter and egg money to buy extra things like Bakers chocolate to make fudge. Here's what Bettina would make herself for Valentine's Day if she wasn't so dern busy with all her homemaking chores.

PIN MONEY FUDGE
Handwritten 1930s Cook Book

4 sq. Bakers chocolate	1 cup rich milk (whole milk)
½ cup cold water	1 tablespoon butter
2 cups granulated sugar	1 tsp. vanilla

"Place the cut-up chocolate and cold water in a unburned saucepan. Stir over low fire till chocolate melts. Remove from fire and stir till smooth. Stir sugar gradually and add milk. Then stir over fire until sugar dissolves. Boil over medium flame to soft ball stage, 235°. Add butter. Put pan in cold water to cool 2 minutes. Add vanilla and broken nut meats if desired. Stir till the fudge thickens and loses shine. Pour into a damp candy tin." (1930s)

Author's note: Pour into a buttered 8 x 8 dish. This depression-era recipe calls for water, so it's inclined to crystallize. You can try omitting the water and decreasing the chocolate to 2 or 3 squares. Let sit 10 minutes after taking off stove, then add vanilla and nuts if you like and stir until no longer glossy.

MONTH OF FEBRUARY

HOT APPLE CUP TARTS
Practical Recipes, 1909

"Use puff-paste, rolling very thin. Have oval-bottomed tin cups, turn cups upside down, lay paste over them, covering them all, cutting around edge of cup. Lay upside down in baking pan and bake to light brown in moderate oven." (1909)

Applesauce for Apple Cups:

"Six apples, brown sugar, good lump of butter, rind and juice of half a fresh lemon. Cook 30 minutes. Keep hot until you wish to serve, adding a little grated nutmeg the last thing. Fill pastry cups with this mixture and on the top, add teaspoon of whipped cream." (1909)

TOLLAND CUP (MAPLE FLAVORED COFFEE)
Mrs Allen's Cook Book, 1917

"To each service allow from 2 to 3 tablespoonfuls of maple syrup, and ¾ cup coffee of medium strength. Let stand to become very cold. Serve in tall, slender glasses, garnish with whipped cream, sweetened with maple syrup, and sprinkled with scraped maple sugar." (1917)

Equal Rights for Jitney Chicks, 1918

City women now operate jitneys, trolleys, elevators, work in machine shops, foundries, and munition plants, besides all the other classes of work they formerly did. Country women are doing their bit in garden, field, and dairy. Almost every farmer's wife or daughter runs the automobile. Some have donned "woman alls" and run tractor, engine, mower, hay rake, etc. Why shouldn't they vote, too? I favor the amendment to the federal constitution providing equal suffrage. So many states now have it, why not all? This era calls for nothing less than equal rights.

~Farm and Home, February, 1918

MONTH OF FEBRUARY

Maidie's Georgia Banana Pudding
Farm & Home, April, 1932

"Cut four bananas in rings and place in layers in a pudding dish, alternating with layers of vanilla wafers. Make a custard sauce of one cupful of milk, one cupful of water, two tablespoonfuls of cornstarch, rubbed smooth with two tablespoonfuls of sugar and pinch of salt, adding one egg and piece of butter the size of a walnut. Cook custard in double-boiler until thick, stirring constantly to make it smooth. Now pour this sauce over the bananas and wafers, lifting them with a fork, so that the custard may run in among the layers. Cover the top with marshmallows and place in the oven until golden brown." (1932)

Author's note: Extra good! Use all milk, increase sugar to ¼ cup, add a tsp. of vanilla after it's thickened. Marshmallows??? Just crumble cookies over top.

Vanilla Wafers
The Boston Cooking School Cook Book, 1898

⅓ cup each butter and lard   2½ cups flour
1 cup sugar   2 teapoons baking powder
1 egg   ½ teaspoon salt
¼ cup milk   2 teaspoons vanilla

"Cream the butter, add sugar, egg well beaten, milk, and vanilla. Mix and sift dry ingredients and add to first mixture. Chill thoroughly. Toss one-fourth of mixture on a floured board and roll as thinly as possible; shape with a small round cutter, first dipped in flour. Place near together on a buttered sheet and bake in a moderate oven. Gather up the trimmings and roll with another portion of dough. During rolling, the bowl containing mixture should be kept in a cool place, or it will be necessary to add more flour to dough, which makes cookies hard rather than crisp and short." (1898)

Author's note: Omit lard and use two-thirds cup butter, decrease milk to 2 Tbs., and only use 1 tsp. baking powder and 1 tsp. vanilla. Roll into logs and chill. Slice thinly and bake at 350° until edges brown lightly.

Blood Orange Curd Thumbprints: For a real treat, press thumb into dough and fill with blood orange curd (page 85) before baking.

RESOURCES

PRODUCTS & SUCH

Brinser's Best Roasted Corn Meal .... www.americanspice.com
Dried Posole (Hominy Corn) & Heirloom Beans
 Rancho Gordo .... www.ranchogordo.com
Citrus-Infused Olive Oil .... www.marinacolonna.it
Heirloom Grains, including buckwheat:
 Anson Mills .... www.ansonmills.com
King Arthur Flour .... www.kingarthurflour.com
Decorative tube cake pans:
 Sur La Table .... www.surlatable.com
Hand Cranked & Electric Grain Mills:
 Lehman's non-electric .... www.lehmans.com
 Pleasant Hill .... www.pleasanthillgrain.com
Lodge Cast Iron Cookware & Dutch Ovens .... www.lodgemfg.com
Home Cheese Making, Riki Carroll .... www.cheesemaking.com
MaryJane's Farm (publications) .... www.maryjanesfarm.com
Slow Food International .... www.slowfood.org
Slow Food USA .... www.slowfoodusa.org

GARDENING

Canning and Preserving .... Ball Blue Book of Preserving
Community Supported Agriculture (CSA) .... www.localharvest.org/csa
Community Gardens:
American Community Garden Assoc. .... www.communitygarden.org
Gleaning Society of St. Andrew .... www.endhunger.org
Heirloom Vegetable Seeds:
Seed Savers Exchange .... www.seedsavers.org
Native Seeds/S.E.A.R.C.H .... www.nativeseeds.org
Ronniger Potato Farm (mail order) .... www.ronnigers.com

RECOMMENDED COOKING CLASSES

John C. Campbell Folk School .... www.folkschool.org
Log Cabin Cooking (author's classes) .... www.nativegroundmusic.com
Swannanoa School of Culinary Arts .... www.schoolofculinaryarts.org

THANKS!

here do I begin? How about with the book cover. Thanks to Steve Millard for turning very ragged vintage cookbook art into an arresting cover. Dudley Wilson and Joe Baum contributed really cool 19th century cookbooks. Thanks to David Battle for the fabulous plums and also to my fruit pilfering partners, Rita Erbsen and Brookes Wolfe. Other fruit picking friends were Jennifer Thomas, Fred and Susan Barbour. Recipe contributors included Pam Budd, Cathy Cleary, Gianluca DeBacco, Leon Swell, and Brookes Wolfe. Editing thanks goes to Janet Swell and Mark Wingate. Jennifer Thomas is my recipe editor, tireless recipe consultant and her popovers really pop. Recipe testers included Annie Erbsen, Rita Erbsen, Marti Otto, Richard Renfro, Renate Rikkers, Liz Swann, Janet Swell, Jennifer Thomas, Courtney Webb, Sara Webb and Laura Wright. Thanks to my Aunt Lila Swell and Sandy Stevenson for research support, and to Betty Sharpless for her inspiration.

Now for the taste-testers. There were a lot of them, basically everybody I know. Our office staff, Kelli Stewart and John Miller were forced to eat an awful lot of cake. Other tasters included Randy Greenberg, Bonnie Neustein, my kids Annie, Wes, and Rita, Jennifer, Cece and Neil Thomas, my sisters, Janet and Laura, and my parents, Nancy and Leon Swell. And to Wayne Erbsen, thanks for your ever-dependable appetite, and encouragement to finish this dern book when I was more interested in playing in my garden than in writing about it.

This book is dedicated to my parents, Nancy and Leon Swell, both extraordinary gardeners and scientists. They inspired me to love native plants and their habitats, and to be curious about all kinds of things like bacteria, fungi, and fern spores. My mother passed away in June of 2008, just as the squash blossoms set. She leaves behind a magnificent native plant garden in Richmond, Virginia, that she and my dad created, and that he still tends.

I didn't have much appetite as a kid, but from my family I learned that everybody shows up for dinner. Hungry or not. And even though the food is what brings us to the table, it's the coming together of loved ones at the end of a long day to chat and share that counts.

BIBLIOGRAPHY

PERIOD BOOKS

A Cookbook for Victory, Immanuel Woman's Club, 1944
A Thousand Ways to Please a Husband With Bettina's Best Recipes,
    Louise Bennett Weaver & Helen Cowles LeCron, 1916
A Thousand Ways to Please a Family, Weaver & LeCron, 1922
Around the Year in the Garden, A Seasonable Guide and Reminder,
    for Work With Vegetables & Fruits, Frederick Rockwell, 1911
Aunt Mary's New England Cook Book, A New England Mother, 1881
Aunt Babette's Cook Book, Aunt Babette, 1889
Calendar of Desserts, Elizabeth O. Hiller, 1910ish
Calendar of Salads, Elizabeth O. Hiller, 1910ish
Calendar of Sandwiches and Beverages, Elizabeth O. Hiller, 1910ish
Chester County Recipes, 19teens
Cyclopedia of American Agriculture, Edited by LH Bailey, 1911
Farmer's Guide and Household Hints, Snow King, 1938
Fruit Recipes, Riley Maria Fletcher Berry, 1906
Good Living, A Practical Cookery Book for Town & Country, Sara Van
    Buren, 1890
Grandma Keeler's Housekeeper, Grandma Keeler, 1912
Guide for Nut Cookery, Almeda Lambert, 1899
How to do Things, Farm Journal, 1919
I Go A-Marketing, Henrietta Sowle, 1900
Making the Farm Pay, Calvin Bowsfield, 1914
McNess Cook Book, McNess Spice Company, 1920
Mother Earth's Children, Elizabeth Gordon, 1914
Mrs. Allen's Cook Book, Ida Bailey Allen, 1917
North American Seasonal Cook Book, Mrs. Anna B. Scott, 1921
Practical Recipes, Mrs. B.B. Cutter, 1909
Sovereign Woman vs. Mere Man, Jennie Day Haines, 1905
The Boston Cooking School Cook Book, Fannie Merritt Farmer, 1896
The Children's Friend, Mormon Church, 1909
The Farmer's Every-Day Book, John L. Blake, 1850
The Farmers and Emigrants Complete Guide, 1856
The Needlework Guild Cook Book, Mrs. Cyrus Jones, 1907
The New Household Receipt-Book, Sarah Hale , 1853
The New Onion Culture, T. Greiner, 1903

BIBLIOGRAPHY

PERIOD BOOKS

The Peanut Plant, Its Cultivation & Uses, B.W. Jones of Va., 1885
The Picayune Creole Cook Book, Times-Picayune Pub. Co., 1922
The Pure Food Cook Book, Harvey Wiley, Mildred Maddockks, 1914
The Rural Cook Book: Published by *The Rural New-Yorker*, 1907
The Stag Cook Book: Written for Men by Men, Carroll Sheridan, 1922
The Successful Housekeeper, Ellsworth and Dickerson, 1887
The Tree Book, Julia Ellen Rogers, 1906
Uncooked Foods, Mr. & Mrs. Eugene Christian, 1904
Unfired Foods and Tropho-Therapy, George Drews, 1910
Weather Opinions for All Seasons, Jennie Day Haines, 1907
What to Have for Luncheon, Mrs. Mary J. Lincoln 1904
When Mother Lets Us Help, Constance Johnston, 1916
When Mother Lets Us Cook, Constance Johnston, 1908
When Mother Lets Us Garden, Frances Duncan, 1918
Ye Gardeyne Boke, Jennie Day Haines, 1906

AGRICULTURAL JOURNALS 1870s-1930s

American Fruit Grower
Country Home
Farm and Fireside
Farm and Home
Farm Journal and Farmer's Wife
Farm Life
Hagers-town Almanack 1929
Old Farmer's Almanac
Rural Life
Rural New-Yorker
Southern Field and Fireside
Southern Ruralist
Successful Farming
The Housewife
The Modern Priscilla
The People's Home Journal
Woman's Farm Journal

Broad beans in the field.

RECIPE INDEX

RECIPE INDEX